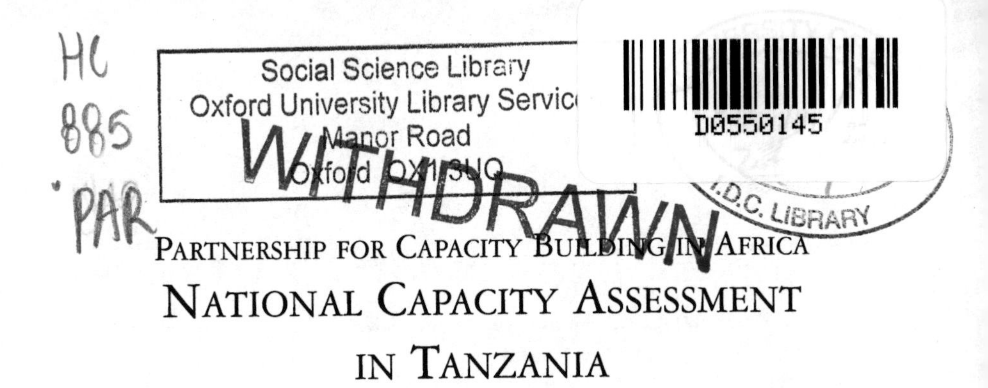

Partnership for Capacity Building in Africa

National Capacity Assessment in Tanzania

Edited by
Professor Samuel M Wangwe
Economic and Social Research Foundation

Mkuki na Nyota Publishers
Dar es Salaam

Published for the Economic and Social Research Foundation by
Mkuki na Nyota Publishers
6 Muhonda Street, Mission Quarter, Kariakoo
P.O. Box 4246, Dar es Salaam
Tanzania

ISBN 9976 973 98 5

Distributed outside Africa by
African Books Collective Ltd
27 Park End Street
Oxford OX1 1HU
UK
www.africanbookscollective.com

TABLE OF CONTENTS

List of Tables v
Abbreviations and Acronyms vi
Introduction 1

1. National Capacity Assessment in Tanzania: An Analysis 3
   The Existing Levels of Capacity 3
   Constraints to Capacity Building 8
   Possible Responses 11
   Problems and Opportunities Related to Donor Intervention 14
   Conclusion 16

2. Financial and Economic Management in the Public Sector 19
   Introduction 19
   Public Sector 19
   Strategy for Capacity Building in Government Economic Management 20
   Planning Commission 20
   Bureau of Statistics 24
   Ministry of Finance 27
   Tanzania Revenue Authority (TRA) 33
   The Exchequer and Audit Department 34
   Land Management 35
   Conclusions 35

3. Capacity of the Civil Service in Tanzania: An Assessment 37
   Introduction 37
   Overall Context of Civil Service Capacity 37
   Existing Capacity, Problems and Constraints of Human Resources in the Civil Service 39
   Civil Service: Organisation and Management Practices 43
   Possible Responses to Problems and Constraints 48
   Conclusion 49

4. Local and Regional Administration in Tanzania 51
   Regional Administration 51
   Local Administration 51
   Existing Level of Capacity 52
   Capacity Building: What is to be done 56
   The Role of Donors 45

5. Capacity in the Private Sector 59
Introduction 59
Constraints to Capacity Building in the Private Sector 60
NGOs and Civic Groups 65

6. Primary and Secondary Education and Vocational Training 66
The Current Situation 67
Problems and Constraints to Capacity Building in Basic Education 74
Responses to the Problems and Constraints 75
Problems and Opportunities Related to Donor Interventions 76

7. Tertiary Education and Training Capacity 79
Major Issues 79
Areas Requiring Corrective Action and Donor Support 84

References 87
Bibliography 89
Appendix: Members of the National Assessment Team for Tanzania 92

LIST OF TABLES

Table 1: Statistical Staff by Level of Education 25

Table 2: Accountant General Department Staff Development Programme (1995/96-1997/98) 31

Table 3: Growth in Civil Service Employment 1961-1994 39

Table 4: Distribution of Government Employees according to Major Occupational Groups 40

Table 5: Distribution of Employees in Functional Groups according to Highest Level of Formal Education (Tanzania) 41

Table 6: Distribution of Employees in Professional and Technical/Associated Professional Related Jobs with Inadequate Skills (Tanzania) 42

Table 7: Fall in Real Wages for Civil Service Employees (1969-1984) 45

Table 8: Minimum and Top Civil Service Basic Salaries in Real Terms (1976 prices) 1984/85-1995/96 46

Table 9: Training Requirements and Actual Disbursement in Local Government Service Commission 56

Table 10: Primary Education Pupils 68

Table 11: Permanent Buildings and Furniture in Primary Schools in 1994 69

Table 12: Primary School Leavers and Form I Selections 1963-1995 71

Table 13: Transition to A-Level 73

Table 14: Transition from Std. VII to A-Level 73

Table 15: Annual University Enrolments in some Eastern, Central and Southern African Countries 80

Table 16: Trends in Female Enrolment in Education and Training Programmes in Proportion to Male Enrolment 1971-95 (%) 81

Table 17: Government Allocation to the University of Dar es Salaam, Tanzania (1985/86-1995/96) 82

ABBREVIATIONS AND ACRONYMS

ACCA	Association of Certified Chartered Accountants
AMACS	Aid Management and Administration Co-ordination Systems
AMAP	Aid Management and Accountability Programme
BEST	Basic Education Statistics in Tanzania
BMDP	Budget Management Development Programme
BS	Bureau of Statistics
CPA	Certified Public Accountant
CRE	Central Register of Establishment
CRSP	Civil Service Reform Programme
CSC	Civil Service Commission
CVCP	Committe of Vice-Chancellors and Principals
DC	District Commissioner
DDC	District Development Corporation
DFID	Department for International Development
EEC	European Economic Community
ESAURP	Eastern and Southern African Universities Research Programme
GDP	Gross Domestic Product
GS	Government Scales
IDM	Institute of Development Management
IFM	Institute of Finance Management
IRDP	Institute of Rural Development Planning
ITA	Institute of Tax Administration
JAAC	Joint Academic Affairs Committee
KAMUS	Kamati za Ajira Serikalini (Government Employment Committees)
LGSC	Local Government Service Commission
M.A.	Masters degree
MIT	Ministry of Industries and Trade
MOLG	Ministry of Local Government
MSTHE	Ministry of Science, Technology and Higher Education
NACP	National Aids Control Programme
NBAA	National Board of Accountants and Auditors
NER	Net Enrolment Ratio
NGOs	Non-Governmental Organisations
NHLMAC	National Higher Level Manpower Allocation Committee
NMS	National Master Sample
OS	Ordinary Scales
Ph.D.	Doctor of Philosophy
PMO	Prime Minister's Office
PROMIS	Project Management Information System
R&D	Research and Development

RC	Regional Commissioner
RDC	Regional Development Corporation
RDD	Regional Development Director
RPFB	Rolling Plan and Forward Budget
RSOs	Regional Statistical Offices
SIDA	Swedish International Development Agency
SUA	Sokoine University of Agriculture
TANGO	Tanzania Non-Governmental Organisations
TET	Tanzania Economic Trend
TRA	Tanzania Revenue Authority
TSC	Teachers Service Commission
Tshs	Tanzania Shillings
UCLAS	University College of Lands and Architectural Studies
UDSM	University of Dar es Salaam
UNDP	United Nations Development Programme
UNICEF	United Nations Children's Fund
UPE	Universal Primary Education
URT	United Republic of Tanzania
USAID	United States Aid for International Development
USD	United States Dollar
VETA	Vocational Education and Training Authority

INTRODUCTION

Capacity comprises human resources and institutions that enable a country to achieve its development goals. Among the numerous causes underlying Africa's poor economic performance, inadequacy in human and institutional capacity is perhaps the most fundamental. It was against this background that the African Governors of the World Bank raised the issue during the Bank's annual meeting in October 1995. The Bank agreed to sponsor a series of sub-regional workshops around Africa with a view to gathering ideas on ways to build capacity.

Workshops bringing together persons with a wide range of expertise — drawn from government, the private sector, academia, NGOs and professional associations — were held in Addis Ababa, Abidjan, Libreville and Johannesburg in March and April 1996. As a result, it was decided that National Capacity Assessment Teams should be formed in 13 African countries, in order to identify strategic capacity needs. Tanzania was one of the countries included. Following the regional workshops, Tanzania formed the National Capacity Assessment Team for this study. The list of the names and designations of the members appears in the Appendix at the end of this report.

The national capacity assessment team agreed that capacity weaknesses exist in virtually all areas of the Tanzanian economy and that capacity issues are complex and interlinked. Because various areas of capacity building are interlinked, interventions to address capacity building in one area must take into account the ways in which capacity in other areas is likely to be affected. It is difficult, for example, to imagine strengthening skills in government agencies for planning, budgeting and implementation without improvements in the quality of professional training available through the education system. Private sector growth requires the development of capable regulatory and judicial institutions and management training as well as access to business information. Thus, policies addressing the capacity issue must look at the wider picture and take account of the ways in which capacity deficits in one sector or area affect capacity in others. These interrelationships are recognised throughout this study.

In order to analyse the issues involved and formulate an appropriate strategy for tackling them, the team identified sectors and areas most in need of capacity assessment. These have been classified into four categories — public sector, private sector, civil society and the education system. The members produced capacity assessment reports for the sectors mentioned, and these have provided the basis for the various chapters of this report.

1. NATIONAL CAPACITY ASSESSMENT IN TANZANIA: AN ANALYSIS

1.1 THE EXISTING LEVELS OF CAPACITY

The existence of capacity gaps is attributed both to low capacity creation and to low utilisation of existing capacity. Skill shortages exist in the country at all levels, from policy analysts and managers to artisans and skilled workers. Lack of trained labour impedes development efforts and economic growth; this in turn reduces revenues and thereby the ability to build capacity. However, because of poor organisation and lack of coherence in institutions, even those scarce skills that are potentially available are not effectively utilised. The combination of inadequate planning, excessive patronage, inadequate reward systems, weak professional institutions and excessive dependence on technical assistance result in a failure to make proper use of available national talent.

1.1.1 Public Sector: Economic Management

With some of the few qualified Tanzanians taking jobs abroad and those remaining obliged to function under adverse working conditions, the country's capacity for strategic thinking and planning has been weakened. Thus, the government takes important actions and implements policy changes without an adequate analysis of the available options or the consequences of a chosen course. In the public sector, reorientation of structures, organisation and skills is required to cope with the redefined role of government in managing a more market-oriented economy in the new era of openness and globalisation. This implies rationalisation of the functions and structure of public institutions, improving organisation and efficiency, pay reform, improving the operational environment and supportive work facilities and organising appropriate training and retraining.

The public institutions responsible for economic policy formulation and financial planning, management and control are the Planning Commission, the Ministry of Finance, the Accountant General's Office in the Ministry of Finance, the Controller and Auditor General's Office and the Revenue Authority.

In the area of economic policy formulation, the Planning Commission has started to shift its attention from investment planning to policy analysis; the productive results of this shift have yet to be realised fully. The responsibility for financial planning, management and control centres on the Ministry of Finance, the Revenue Authority and the Exchequer and Auditor General's Office. The Ministry lacks the necessary staff to carry out its crucial responsibilities in managing the nation's finances; in particular, the Accountant General's Office is understaffed.

The Revenue Authority is an independent Government agency operating outside the civil service framework. It has however inherited many weaknesses from the system it replaced in the areas of staff, equipment and systems.

The Exchequer and Auditor General's Office employs about 350 managerial and technical staff, but relatively few of these possess acceptable audit qualifications. The department lacks adequate work facilities.

The quality of the information system for economic data is an important element in developing the capacity for economic and policy analysis. The capacity of the Bureau of Statistics needs to be revamped. Most staff members of the Bureau need to update/improve their technical and managerial skills. They need specialised training to increase knowledge of statistical methods, to enhance economic literacy and knowledge of national accounting, and to improve computer skills. The Bureau needs to upgrade the competence of the 20 regional statistical offices (RSOs), of which only three are currently headed by statisticians.

Capacity building for public economic management should address:

(a) macroeconomic and sectoral policy formulation, implementation and monitoring under market-oriented conditions;
(b) improving the system of social and economic data collection, processing and dissemination, taking into account changes in the economic environment;
(c) public finance management, especially revenue assessment and collection and control and monitoring of public expenditure;
(d) central and local government capacity for carrying out assessment of communities' needs for promoting locally-based community development;
(e) capacity for negotiations with international agencies and countries and for follow-up of programmes under co-operation agreements; and
(f) mechanisms for positive dialogue and co-operation between the public and private sectors.

1.1.2 Civil Service

The civil service in Tanzania greatly expanded over the years, from about 90,000 people in 1961 to about 316,000 in 1994. Of these civil servants, professionals and administrators represent 5%, while middle-level technicians and lower cadres represent the remaining 95%. In 1988, about 60% of the civil servants had an educational level of up to primary school only. Earlier studies suggested that 44% of civil servants were assigned duties for which they had no skills and that 51% of the civil servants assigned supervisory and administrative responsibilities at various levels did not possess the required background.

Civil service training capacity is low due to lack of adequate teaching staff, systematic training programmes and teaching facilities. To enhance capacity in this sector, training should consider and include:

(a) skills for managing private sector participation in the economy to ensure a fair conduct of business by the private sector;
(b) ability of the government to manage the interests of the various groups in the society and at the same time enhancing their capacities for locating their interests in the broader context of interests of the society at large;
(c) capacity for keeping abreast of fast-changing technology; and
(d) policies ensuring that all areas of the public service are staffed by enough qualified people.

1.1.3 LOCAL ADMINISTRATION

Capacity building in local government poses the challenges of training and retraining staff to cope with greater responsibilities of development management. All the three levels of the local administration — namely councils, wards and villages — require revamping in terms of equipment, staff and revenue-collection capacity. These efforts should focus on:

(a) administrative capacity to facilitate attainment of development objectives, namely the ability of staff to comprehend and interpret government policies and understand the scope of their responsibilities at the regional level, as well as ability to maintain peace, order and good government and promote social welfare and economic well-being at the local level;
(b) revenue collection and utilisation;
(c) planning and programme evaluation;
(d) tax assessment; and
(e) manpower planning and incentive package.

1.1.4 PRIVATE SECTOR

The private sector in Tanzania is fragile due to many factors, including:

(a) a banking and financial system that includes a large and fragile State-owned segment;
(b) uncertainty about the direction and the sustainability of the macroeconomic policy framework;
(c) apprehension about the genuineness of government's ideological shift to favour the private sector;

(d) the declining standards of education at all levels, absence of an equity capital market; and
(e) technological obsolescence.

Informal sector entrepreneurs lack the business and marketing skills to grow beyond small-scale operation and are further frustrated by bureaucratic obstacles and uncertainties in support services. Important possible initiatives include:

(a) formation of a strong and sustainable national forum to facilitate dialogue between the government and the business community;
(b) establishment of venture capital financing institutions;
(c) development of entrepreneurial capacity through appropriate education and training;
(d) promotion of research-and-development (R&D) projects and programmes;
(e) establishment of an operational stock market to encourage broader ownership of enterprises;
(f) creation of an enabling policy environment for the private sector; and
(g) sensitisation of the general public to the potential contribution of the private sector, as well as to the role of co-operatives as engines of private sector development, especially in the rural areas.

1.1.5 CIVIL SOCIETY

Capacity building in the Non-Governmental Organisation sector needs to recognise that the NGOs play an increasingly important social role in the country. People are creating new institutions to provide for needs that are not being met by either the market or the public sector. Formation of NGOs is in part a response to a declining capacity of the government to meet its obligations, particularly in delivery of services not appropriate to the private sector. Service institutions have sprung up which are not government agencies but are not profit-making. However, thus far little or no attention has been paid to this sector, in terms of its economics, management, performance and impact. One reason may be the extremely heterogeneous character of the sector.

The existing capacity of NGOs is inadequate. Local NGOs are weak, and a number of NGOs operating in the country are agents of international NGOs, which limits autonomy in priority setting, and can hinder the development of local capacity. There is a tendency to concentrate on activities that can attract external support rather than on those reflecting local priorities.

NGOs need the capacity to mobilise and inform their constituencies, to reflect constituencies' needs and aspirations and to communicate and negotiate with government and private sector interlocutors.

1.1.6 THE EDUCATION SYSTEM

Education has been neglected at every level and effective access to quality education is limited for a large part of the population. Both the access and quality of primary education have deteriorated. The quality and relevance of secondary and tertiary education is generally unsatisfactory and, combined with a shortage of vocational and technical training, it has led to an under-skilled workforce. The schools and universities are producing large numbers of graduates without the requisite skills for performing adequately in the public and private sectors.

Currently there are 11,630 primary schools in Tanzania with a total pupil population of 4,382,410 in 2001 — this number has risen from about 3,400,000 in 1990. However, most of these schools suffer from a shortage of qualified teachers as well as inadequate teaching facilities and materials, particularly in the rural areas.

In the area of secondary education, there were 927 ordinary level secondary schools in 2001 (400 private and 527 public) with about 184,000 students. Student intake capacity at the secondary school level and vocational training level is low. Teaching staff and facilities require improvement in both public and private schools.

Enrolment capacity and funding are extremely low at the tertiary education level. There has been an imbalance in intake between the humanities and liberal arts on one hand and the sciences and science-based subjects on the other by a tilt of 1/0.5 against the sciences. Gender balance is conspicuously tilted in favour of male students at the university level, particularly in technical subjects.

Primary and secondary education curricula need to be adjusted to reflect recent social and economic developments in the country. The recent classification for secondary schools according to career paths needs to be effectively implemented. The search for quality, which has been reflected in the current move towards privatisation of education delivery systems, needs to be met by improved facilities, including better-trained and motivated teaching staff, improved basic infrastructure and teaching materials.

In the area of tertiary education, the issues to be examined should include the following: enrolment levels; female representation; allocation of funds; co-ordination of the tertiary institutions; teaching methodology; student output (numbers and relevance for employment); and the improvement of incentive structure for capacity retention.

1.1.7 CROSS-CUTTING ISSUES

The following three broad areas cut across the sectors:

- Professionalism: Developing capacity means making professionalism the norm for work performance in government ministries and public enterprises as well as the private sector. It also implies standards of workplace behaviour that are goal-oriented, merit-based and untainted by personal connections or patronage.

- Institutional Autonomy: Institutional autonomy refers to the ability of staff to go about their duties unhindered by political or personal requests for favours.
- Managerial Effectiveness: Sound management requires good leadership, as well as effective external relations and internal administration, maintenance of autonomy and the management of technical assistance in such a manner that the objectives set are achieved with minimum cost.

1.2 CONSTRAINTS TO CAPACITY BUILDING

1.2.1 HUMAN RESOURCES

Capacity building in Tanzania has been driven more by donor supply than by internal demand and strategic planning. It is important that the national leadership takes responsibility for the country's capacity-building efforts. This will involve added commitment on the part of the leadership to taking initiative in capacity building, rallying support for the effort among national constituencies and utilising potential capacity effectively. The government needs to articulate a vision for national development.

The number of available trained and skilled economic analysts, development managers, engineers, accountants, and other professionals needed to perform the tasks of leading and managing the national development process is insufficient. This is largely a consequence of low investment in human resources at all the levels of the education system; however it also results from failure to develop skills on the job.

Tanzania's shortage of technical and managerial capacity has brought with it a chronic dependency on external technical assistance, which displaces rather than develops national capacity. The few professionals qualified to formulate policy, manage development projects and deal constructively with donors and multilateral institutions have not been used effectively. Policies for fostering an effective mix of local capacity and foreign technical assistance to meet national needs have not been adequate defined either by the government or donors.

After entering the service, government employees receive too little training to prepare them for their responsibilities; they are not properly inducted into their posts and do not receive adequate on-the-job supervision to develop their skills. Staff training programmes have hitherto tended to be unsystematic, and poorly programmed and co-ordinated. In some cases, a few individuals have attended several programmes consecutively and repeatedly, while others do not attend even a single study course in their entire working lives. The training that is offered tends to be supply-driven, classroom-oriented and inadequately focused on job requirements, rather than demand-driven, needs based and practice-oriented. 'In-house' training capacity to tailor training to specific career development objectives does not exist. There are widespread problems of under-utilisation, misallocation and/or job personnel mismatching of civil servants, compounded by inadequate work facilities and an unsatisfactory working environment.

1.2.2 INSTITUTIONAL CAPACITY

Institutional capacity, in terms of a regulatory framework and bureaucracy that are appropriate for economic development, poses a particularly difficult challenge to Tanzanian leaders. Part of this problem has arisen because the institutions inherited from the colonial authorities were not effectively adapted to the needs of an independent state. However, failures of post-colonial governance have undermined the effectiveness of institutions. Unsatisfactory governance — particularly regarding accountability of government officials; transparency in government procedures and processes (e.g., in investment decisions, contracts and appointments); unpredictability in government behaviour; excessive secrecy in government information flows; and nonobservance of the rule of law — have undermined the performance of government and its credibility. Institutional weakness has been reinforced by personalised exercise of authority, which has impeded effective reform, leaving public administration to be excessively influenced by personal connections and patronage networks. The breakdown of key institutions — particularly in education, the civil service, the judiciary system and throughout government and the private sector — has made it difficult for Tanzania to produce capable workers or to use the capacities of the workforce effectively.

The economic difficulties experienced since the mid-1970s severely eroded the earnings of Tanzanian professionals (particularly in the public sector), reduced public revenues and hampered the performance of key capacity-building institutions such as the education system. Poor morale and rent-seeking behaviour in the public sector (due to low pay, lack of a development focus and weak management) have been impeding economic growth at every level.

1.2.3 THE POLICY AND INCENTIVE ENVIRONMENT

Inappropriate macroeconomic policies have not encouraged development. Economic growth has been sluggish and, in a number of years, even negative. Because economic growth and capacity are mutually reinforcing, slow economic growth has had severe implications for the development of the country's human and institutional capacity.

The private sector is constrained by burdensome regulations, unnecessary administrative and bureaucratic requirements, inappropriate and non-functioning legal and judicial frameworks, excessive reliance on public enterprises and the public's stigmatisation of private business. The private sector's energy is further sapped because the principles of good governance have too often been compromised.

The system of universal primary education and vocational training has not been used effectively to increase the potential of workers. Workers who have appropriate basic education are better able to adapt to the demands of a changing work environment. Unfortunately, in recent years the education system has not adequately responded to a national need for capacity building. Average per capita expenditure on primary and secondary school students has declined in real terms. The proportion of children enrolled has also declined, leaving a steadily growing and marginalised school-age population outside of the school system.

In the area of higher education and training institutions there is urgent need to enhance the quality and reach of education and to adjust vocational training to the needs of the economy. Problems in the education system include:

- an imbalance in student enrolment between the humanities and the sciences and science-based subjects;
- low female representation, particularly in higher education;
- under-financing, proliferation and lack of co-ordination of tertiary institutions;
- inadequate strategies to improve teachers' skills; and
- low quality of student output at the higher education and university training levels.

In the past two decades, government has not had the financial resources to support an increased student intake and to maintain standards under existing modes of operation. One outcome, since the early 1980s, has been increasing staff turnover and brain drain.

The quality of communication between the government and the public has been weakened by a long period of over-centralised control, which discouraged free expression of alternative views, tending to isolate political leaders from social demands and public opinion. An over-centralised and ineffective economic policy regime frightened away potential private foreign partners and discouraged the mobilisation of private domestic resources for investment.

On the basis of the current findings of the capacity needs assessment team, there is an urgent need to increase the resources devoted to education, training and research, and to allocate funds on a demand-driven basis. Also the areas of infrastructure, rural development, and health care deserve special attention. However, in all this, success will depend on the commitment of the national leadership to capacity building and the creation of an 'enabling environment' to encourage decentralised initiatives.

1.3 POSSIBLE RESPONSES

1.3.1 Strategic Human Knowledge and Skills

A key need is the development of strategic human knowledge and skills. This requires a focus on institutions providing strategic support services (such as the consulting profession, especially in the areas of financial resource management, strategic planning, information technology, production technology and productive incentives); research institutions; and training for journalists and civic organisations.

Improvements in tertiary education and training should include: increased student enrolments in general (e.g., innovative forms of cost sharing), and also of female students; rationalisation of tertiary education institutions; increased financing of tertiary education institutions; strengthening of teaching-learning improvement units and, within the context of an agreed strategy, giving universities and other training institutions more autonomy in managing their activities.

1.3.2 Transforming Government and its Public Agencies

To be successful, development efforts in Tanzania must be accompanied by a transformation of the role of government and the public sector. The responsibilities of government should be narrowed, to concentrate on those activities necessarily the responsibility of the State, and a systematic effort should be made to do those tasks well. With a more focused agenda, it should be possible to strengthen government institutions through improved management, greater administrative freedom from political interference, and incentive systems that increase staff motivation. It should be possible to streamline and professionalise core functions — with an emphasis on the delivery of quality services — and to promote good governance through training, introduction of professional auditing standards and elimination of unethical practices. There is also a need to increase government capacity for economic policy analysis and development (particularly financial) management.

The strategy for capacity building in the public sector should ensure that capacity-building programmes are internalised in the various public institutions, particularly in relation to the rationalisation of their functions and structures.

The Government has embarked on a Civil Service Reform Programme which seeks to transform the civil service in its role, functions and structures as well as to improve its skills and capacity to make them relevant and consistent with the redefined policies and strategies for national economic development and with the delivery of public services which are predicated on a vastly enhanced role of the private sector. The key features of this programme, which should be continued, include the following:

(a) reducing the role and functions of the government, not only by the government divesting itself of activities but also by systematically exploring options and alternative mechanisms for delivery of services that the government currently provides;
(b) improving the quality, motivation, morale and performance of civil servants to enhance service delivery with fewer public servants;
(c) decentralising delivery of functions and services to local government councils, autonomous and self-financing government agencies, Non-Governmental Organisations and community-based organisations; and
(d) contracting out non-core and auxiliary services to private sector operators.

Government should focus its attention on administration, law and order, on basic services which cannot be provided adequately by the private sector (particularly social services, communications infrastructure and public utilities), on provision of an enabling environment for the private sector, and on public sector financial management.

The Planning Commission, as the lead government economic advisory agency, should focus on macroeconomic policy formulation and analysis, sectoral policies/strategy formulation and analysis, economic research, private sector development and dialogue, and statistical analysis, interpretation and presentation. The strategy of capacity building for the Planning Commission should focus on:

(a) training of macro- and sectoral-economic and policy economists and other experts like statisticians, environmentalists, sociologists, etc.;
(b) training in statistical research, analysis and modelling techniques;
(c) development of policy-research capacities and links through team-work with other research agencies within the country and through selective working attachments in other ministries, financial institutions and international agencies;
(d) development and promotion of modalities for promoting dialogue with the private sector and for developing positive alliance with the sector;
(e) introduction of appropriate computer networks and logistical support to facilitate networking with other centres of information and ideas; and
(f) creation of an improved environment for analytical work within the civil services, including improved working conditions and supervision.

The Ministry of Finance should develop capacity in the formulation of overall policies in revenue collection, budget preparation and management, external finance management, government accounting systems and procedures and payroll computerisation. The Exchequer and Audit Department needs strengthening in basic auditing skills, managerial knowledge, equipment and systems. Land management is another important area requiring capacity building, especially given that the private sector is being called upon to provide a lead in the country's economic growth. Areas that need attention include improvement of human resource and institutional capabilities and relevance, improving land access for development agencies and businesses; and putting in place a transparent land allocation system.

1.3.3 Strengthening Private Sector Capacity

To transform national resources and maximise the opportunities from wealth creating markets, the private sector must be strengthened. This includes the ability to take over activities divested by government and convert them into a more profitable and productive basis. This requires strengthening private sector management skills as well as accounting practices and marketing skills, increasing access to business information and attracting and utilising skilled Tanzanians now residing abroad. Key areas for enhancing the country's entrepreneurial capacity include:

- the provision of training to nascent small and medium-scale entrepreneurs;
- putting in place adequate venture capital financing institutions;
- the development of broad ownership of privatised State-owned enterprises and of the large family-owned businesses through an operational stock market;
- reorientation of the education system to make it more responsive to private sector needs; and
- increasing access to relevant technologies and export market information — in the age of globalisation, the capacity to access and apply relevant technologies and export markets information and meet international standards of quality and price is crucial for export growth.

Developing national confidence in the private sector, which in the past has been viewed as an instrument of exploitation and enrichment by a racial minority, is a critical element in building capacity of the private sector. A deliberate move towards the establishment of publicly held companies, and away from exclusively family-owned enterprises, would significantly help to develop a more positive attitude towards the private sector. Private sector capacity would be enhanced by:

- improved policy dialogue between the government and the business sector;
- a development vision that clearly articulates the ideological path of the country's development;
- a legal and regulatory regime that is responsive to, and supportive of, a new market-oriented environment;
- a bureaucracy that is sufficiently sensitive and responsive to private sector led development; and
- allocation of public resources to promoting private sector growth and viability.

A strong formal national forum for dialogue between the government and the business sector could make an important contribution to building capacity in the private sector.

1.3.4 STRENGTHENING NGOS AND CIVIC GROUPS

Social development in Tanzania needs to be supported by serious efforts to strengthen the capacity of communities to manage their own affairs, by support for community-based initiatives and by strengthening linkages between the informal and formal economies. Such actions could contribute to sustained poverty reduction. This requires enhancing the organisational, managerial and technical capacity of community groups and NGOs for policy advocacy and delivery of services to their members and/or clientele. This includes increasing the capacity of civic organisations for partnership with government and donors, and to formulate their goals and implement and evaluate programmes. NGOs and the various civic groups have not performed satisfactorily because of such factors as shortage of funds and technical know-how, and inadequate public outreach.

1.4. PROBLEMS AND OPPORTUNITIES RELATED TO DONOR INTERVENTION

1.4.1 PROBLEMS

1.4.1.1 *Aid Planning and Administration*

In principle, Tanzania has evolved an elaborate structure to negotiate and manage foreign aid, centring on the Planning Commission and the Ministry of Finance. Nevertheless, the aid planning and implementation process has tended to be ad hoc and to be heavily dominated by the donors and their policies. As a result, there is a lack of national ownership of aid programmes, which tends to result in weak commitment to them.

There is a lack of focused strategies to deal with capacity weaknesses revealed in the aid relationship, and a continued dependence on foreign technical assistance personnel in project design and implementation. Multilateral agencies and bilateral donors tend to adopt supply-driven approaches reflecting their own bureaucratic needs rather than developing projects that reflect local realities and conform to a national development vision based on assessment of real needs. Donors often have to operate on such internally imposed, tight schedules that the involvement of local capacity in the project process is either compromised altogether or ineffectively engaged. The observance of deadlines has taken precedence over consultation, and mobilisation of local capacity to design and process projects.

1.4.1.2 *Co-ordination of Aid*

While paying lip service to the need for capacity building, in practice donors generally have not taken the capacity problem seriously. It is easier to bypass national institutions and rely on outside experts in pursuit of the short-term goals of designing projects to meet their own criteria and disbursing funds rather than ensuring project sustainability or laying the foundation for sustained long-term development.

As a result, many programmes are operated with little consultation and co-ordination with related activities within government, even within the same ministry or department. Confused and unco-ordinated donor programmes place further pressure on the already overburdened human and institutional capacities, instead of contributing to capacity building.

Faced with capacity constraints, typical donor responses have been to try to bypass them with ad hoc project-based arrangements, which add to the incoherence of the overall incentive system. Special units within projects have led to continued dependency, added to overall project costs, undermined morale and have failed to create capacity that could be sustained after the life of the projects. To staff project units, donors hire qualified civil servants by offering them salaries and incentive packages that government ministries cannot match, thereby undermining the capacity of public institutions.

The principal donor approach to capacity building has been technical assistance. The premise was that expatriate experts would train qualified Tanzanian counterparts to take over the tasks that the experts were initially engaged to perform. The donors themselves, however, have basically managed technical assistance, and, typically, few real skill transfers take place. A number of factors help to explain this. Typically technical assistance is not undertaken as part of a coherent national effort to build the human and institutional capacity needed for sustainable development, but has been more a response to short-term project requirements. Local staff are not involved in project design. Extremely high remuneration differences between local staff and expatriate staff undermine co-operative relationships. Local personnel often have limited access to project facilities such as vehicles and computers. Counterparts are often appointed late and at an inappropriate level to take over the foreign experts' jobs. Expatriate experts are typically more accountable to the donor than the recipient institution.

Donors have been overloading the policy agenda with an ever-increasing set of issues of concern to donor constituencies, without taking account of the scarcity of government capacity to achieve their goals. This situation has been further aggravated by inadequate donor co-ordination and, sometimes, by competition among donors in the pursuit of their piecemeal, project-based approach. The inter-donor co-ordination that currently exists in Tanzania is largely limited to achieving consensus on policies, especially in relation to economic reform, rather than focused on actual implementation issues.

In summary, in relation to capacity building it is difficult not to conclude that, despite stated commitment, the behaviour of the donor community is currently contributing to the capacity problem rather than contributing to its solution.

1.4.2 OPPORTUNITIES

Offices with donor financed projects are generally better equipped with facilities such as computers, and stand out as 'islands' of well-equipped facilities rather than represent a general improvement in the public service. The challenge is to ensure that improvements through donor support are integrated into the existing structures with a view to raising the overall efficiency and effectiveness of the system.

The greatest opportunity would arise if the World Bank and other donors were to rethink their approach to technical assistance and commit themselves genuinely to local ownership of the capacity-building programmes. Several donors already accept the view that the ultimate responsibility for aid co-ordination should lie with the recipient country. Also, donors have been willing to shift their aid from project aid to programme aid. A number of donors are paying more attention to the need for capacity building within the institutions which are responsible for planning, administration, budgeting and auditing of aid. This greater emphasis on capacity building and increased local responsibility provides as opportunity for Tanzania to articulate and implement new policies in relation to the capacity implications of aid programmes. Aid-funded projects should, in future, be designed and implemented by local institutions wherever possible. Government and donors should avoid funding projects for which adequate design and implementing capacity is lacking. Where existing institutions are too weak to design and implement projects, a substantial capacity-building effort should be mounted before the institution is assigned responsibility for using aid funds.

1.5 CONCLUSION

The Tanzanian environment does not provide an easy context for capacity building. Often Tanzanian leaders find it easier to rely upon foreign technical assistance rather than invest in capacity or utilise that which is already available. The national pool of educated and skilled staff is spread exceedingly thinly and depressing professional conditions make it difficult to motivate employees to exert their most productive efforts. However, ultimately Tanzania's destiny lies in the hands of Tanzanians themselves; they must develop the capacity to formulate, design and implement their own development choices. This suggests that the most realistic policy option should involve the planned phasing down of aid over time.

Three implications are:

(a) putting more emphasis on domestic mobilisation and commitment of resources;
(b) greater utilisation of the local natural and human resources; and
(c) paying more attention to national capacity building, especially in the management of the economy.

Specific activities should include the following:

- Ensuring that the overall capacity of, and relationships between, the different departments of ministries are taken into account at the design stage, and that a programme approach is adopted as far as possible when formulating and designing capacity-building programmes.
- Ensuring that capacity-building programmes address the government's leadership role in national economic management, and as such taking steps to improve policy formulation, monitoring and evaluation capacity.
- Ensuring that donor-supported projects/programmes are located so as to ensure effective operational consultation and co-ordination with related activities.
- In cases where capacity of the host institution is weak, steps should be taken to enhance that capacity, rather than designing projects to operate in parallel structures.
- The current practice of holding annual consultations with each donor separately should be supplemented with sectoral meetings, in which donors to specific sectors would meet under the chairmanship of the Government Ministry in charge of the sector to review progress and, where necessary, redefine sectoral programmes.
- Extending capacity-building initiatives to local government, regional and district administration, community-based organisations and NGOs, with a view to strengthening them and enhancing actual involvement and participation of society in the management of the economy.
- Eliminating the concept of project staff and project experts outside the establishment, to avoid the current practice of instituting parallel administrative structures for projects.
- Ensuring that on-the-job training is approached more comprehensively and systematically, and given greater attention than it is at present, when much emphasis is put on offsite training through scholarships. Training in seminars and workshops should be integrated into comprehensive training programmes, which should make greater use of existing training institutions, rather than establishing new training centres to meet each new need.

- Paying special attention to the civil service reform components, which deal with the working conditions of the civil servants (including remuneration), and integrating the Civil Service Reform Programme with the programme for building capacity in economic management.

The strengthening of local government, community-based organisations and NGOs would contribute to the public's participation in development activities at all levels. Greater efforts should be made towards extending capacity-building initiatives to those levels by preparing a separate programme. This should be facilitated by the process of democratisation and political liberalisation, which has allowed an increase in the role of groups other than the government in policy making and programme implementation. Actors in the private sector and in civil society (NGOs and civic groups) are now able to articulate their positions and interest in various issues, but need help to improve their capacity to articulate their needs and influence policy. The emerging shift from an administrative control towards a market-oriented economy requires the building of capacity for the various responsible groups to participate in such an economy.

2. FINANCIAL AND ECONOMIC MANAGEMENT IN THE PUBLIC SECTOR

2.1 INTRODUCTION

During the late 1970s and early '80s the economy of Tanzania experienced serious problems. Growth was constrained by infrastructural bottlenecks, scarcity of basic commodities, low domestic savings and investment, inadequate and non-competitive banking and financial services. There were persistent budget deficits, exchange rates were overvalued and inflation rose to high levels. The public sector suffered from widespread inefficiency and public service delivery deteriorated. The real wages of public employees declined sharply, resulting in low morale, poor discipline, low productivity and severe weakening of institutional administrative capacity. As a result of taking on too much, the government's capacity to perform was eroded. The proliferation of government activities during the 1970s was, in part, fuelled by indiscriminate donor support.

In a series of reforms implemented in the 1980s, the government reduced indirect economic controls, opened the economy to the private sector and began the process of concentrating its own focus on the traditional functions of government. It increasingly confined its own economic role to areas that could not be adequately serviced by the private sector. The role of the market in directing domestic activities is increasingly important. Thus, new policy environment requires significant changes of techniques and attitudes in the public institutions responsible for managing the economy.

2.2 PUBLIC SECTOR

Public agencies responsible for economic management undertake:

(a) formulation and management of development policies and strategies;
(b) management of the recurrent and investment budgets;
(c) co-ordination of the delivery of social services and public goods;
(d) negotiation with donor agencies; and
(e) formulation of policy for, and promotion of, dialogue with the private sector.

Public institutions, which take the lead in economic policy formulation and implementation of financial management and control, include the Planning Commission, Ministry of Finance and Accountant General, Controller and Auditor General and the Revenue Authority. The Ministry of Lands is also touched on briefly, because lack of secure access to land is a serious impediment to private development.

2.3 STRATEGY FOR CAPACITY BUILDING IN GOVERNMENT ECONOMIC MANAGEMENT.

Capacity building involves the development of individuals through training or retraining, promotion of an improved work environment through provision of equipment and logistical support, more systematic work supervision and career development and appropriate incentive packages. A capacity-building programme should focus on:

(a) re-examining the mission and vision of public institutions;
(b) rationalisation of functions and structure of public institutions in line with the mission and vision;
(c) providing necessary staffing, equipment and logistical support;
(d) improving operational processes and the work environment;
(e) reforming pay packages, providing attractive working schemes combined with appropriate performance checks; and
(f) organising appropriate training and retraining.

2.4 PLANNING COMMISSION

Following the ongoing economic reforms, the role and focus of activities for the Planning Commission has to change to more market-oriented policy formulation, analysis, and research. With this new focus, the Planning Commission is no longer expected to concentrate on investment planning, but to focus on macroeconomic policy formulation and analysis; sectoral policies/strategy formulation and analysis; economic and social problem-solving; and formulation of policies for and promotion of dialogue with the private sector.

A reorientation of the Planning Commission's activities towards policy analysis, planning and monitoring will not diminish the importance of its responsibilities. However, the quality of its analyses — rather than its direct involvement in a variety of administrative processes — would become the main instrument of its influence.

The Commission would need to take the lead in co-ordinating economic intelligence and policy analysis within government, and effectively network with policy research institutions in the country to ensure in-depth analysis of specific policy issues. It should no longer maintain the pretension that it is engaged in 'comprehensive planning' (with the implication that it should have staff to routinely cover all aspects of the economy), but it should be capable of selective problem solving and 'trouble-shooting'.

The Commission should strive to be recognised as the best source of economic intelligence and policy advice in the country. Its role should be to define the common policy agenda of government institutions and donor agencies operating in the country. To play this role its key need, in terms of staff, will not be for large numbers, or even a matter of formal qualifications. Rather it will require a team of high-quality analysts, capable of taking initiative and working innovatively.

2.4.1 EXISTING PROFESSIONAL CAPACITIES

The Planning Commission has about 100 professionals — 60 economists, 12 statisticians, ten manpower specialists, eight planners and ten other professionals. Out of 100 professionals, 45 have Master's degrees or Ph.D.s and 40 have first degrees. Most of the senior managers have diversified professional backgrounds, having worked in other economic management agencies prior to their assignment to the Planning Commission.

2.4.2 CAPACITY CONSTRAINTS

Economic and policy analysis depends on quality, relevance and timeliness in the production of basic economic data. In the context of a deregulated economy, some of the traditional sources of economic information have virtually disappeared. The Bureau of Statistics, and the other Departments of the Commission, can no longer rely on public institutions to provide data relating to agricultural and industrial production, construction, transport, trade and other services, or movements of domestic prices. Addressing the emerging economic environment will require renovation in the system of formal data collection; perhaps, more fundamentally, a change in the style of work will be necessary. Economic policy work is likely to be well informed and relevant only if staff are exposed to economic realities beyond the normal bureaucratic confines. Increasingly, government policy advisors will need to get out and about in the private and informal economies, as well as up country.

In relation to formal data requirements, ongoing reviews have recommended that the Bureau of Statistics should become an autonomous executive agency. The Bureau should operate flexibly, diversify its activities and its clients, work with, and meet the needs of, private enterprises and NGOs, and should also continue to produce reliable statistics on the Tanzanian economy for economic management agencies and policy-makers. A national economic information strategy should be formulated to articulate the main priorities of the Bureau, integrating the Bureau's activities within the framework of an effort by all economic management agencies to produce the type of information and analysis that policy-makers need to perform their policy functions. The proposed information strategy should to improve the quality and timeliness of data production, but also the need to present statistics in a form that politicians and civil servants can understand, even if they lack an economics background. The production of short, user-friendly, economic management documents is essential to influence the policy agenda of the government and the donor community.

Another important capacity constraint is the poor quality of the work environment. Office space, office supplies and equipment are grossly inadequate. The Commission has 28 offices for about 115 managers and other professionals. Much of the equipment is not functioning. A couple of units are supported by externally-funded projects and are better equipped to carry out their main functions. Others are ill-equipped to perform their tasks.

The existing incentive system does not adequately reward competence and performance. The level of salaries in the Planning Commission and the structure of the overall compensation packages (by specialisation, grade and function) should be further reviewed in the context of the pay reform initiated by the Civil Service Reform Programme. This is one area in which it would make sense to dispose of available resources over a much smaller staff, improving both incentives and work environment, to improve the quality of the output.

Available training programmes and staff development policies do not correspond to the new priorities. Professional mobility is an important instrument of staff development for an institution that needs to understand the working of a wide variety of decentralised economic agencies. A new training and staff development strategy for the staff of the Planning Commission needs to be designed and implemented. Staff development strategies should not only improve the technical background and the professional experience of the Commission's professionals, but should also promote attitudes aimed at encouraging interdepartmental co-operation and a better understanding of the economic reality outside government. The Commission will be unable to perform its new role as an effective intermediary between the public and private sector unless its staff develop a broad understanding of developments in the private sector.

2.4.3 STRATEGY FOR CAPACITY BUILDING IN THE PLANNING COMMISSION

The Planning Commission needs a programme of capacity building to change the orientation of its workforce and provide necessary working skills, logistical support and a conducive working environment, focusing on the following items or activities:

(a) training of macro- and sectoral-economic and policy economists and complementary experts such as statisticians, environmentalists, sociologists, etc.;
(b) training in statistical research, analysis and modelling techniques;
(c) development of policy-research capacities and links through team-work with other research agencies within the country, including working attachments in other ministries, financial institutions and international development agencies, and promotion of modalities for dialogue with the private sector and for developing positive alliances with the sector;
(d) secondment of short-term specialists from other ministries, academic institutions and the private sector to tackle priority issues;

(e) introducing appropriate computer networks, then improving staff familiarisation and providing other logistical support to network with other centres of information and ideas;
(f) strengthening the Bureau of Statistics by improving the quality of staff at the head office and regional levels; and
(g) putting in place attractive incentives, working conditions and supervisory arrangements.

2.4.4 Training Programme for the Planning Commission

The Commission should be developed as a centre of excellence, to become the best source of economic intelligence and policy advice in the country. The Planning Commission should be able to take the lead in defining the national policy agenda. To achieve this, a critical input is the training of professionals currently working with the Planning Commission and those who will be recruited on a competitive basis. The selection of those to be trained should be based on proven capacity for analytical work. Based on the new functioning of the Planning Commission, the key need is to develop basic skills in analysis and writing, backed up by a robust rather than over-sophisticated control of techniques.

Sufficient training is required to make professionals confident in their areas of specialisation and to command respect from their domestic and international colleagues. For this purpose, emphasis in recruitment and training should not exaggerate the importance of diplomas and degrees as such, as diplomas are of highly variable quality; rather, attention should be focused on practical evidence of the acquisition of skills. For this purpose, a careful assessment of the level of performance is more important than emphasising that staff should have a Master's or Doctorate degree — which in itself may indicate little.

With the highly competitive job market that now exists, it should be possible to recruit new entrants from among those of best potential. However, in judging this potential and the meaning of subsequent qualifications, the government economic service may need to put in place its own system of assessment of individuals by examination, interview and job-performance assessment.

In terms of formal training, key professionals should normally have a further academic qualification after a general M.A./M.Sc. degree course. For first-degree holders, the goal should be to complete M.A./M.Sc.degrees (although it should be noted that the need for M.A. training itself reflects the deterioration of undergraduate training, so that work done in a Bachelor's course a generation ago is now postponed to the M.A. course). M.A./M.Sc. holders could be exposed to more challenging training at the level of one-year M. Phil. degree courses abroad, or Ph.D. level degrees conducted jointly by the University of Dar es Salaam and foreign universities. Subjects for Ph.D. dissertations should be chosen carefully to reflect topical issues, in relation to which candidates should be exposed to relevant international experience. In addition to formal training, in-service short-term courses should be offered. These should both tackle specialised policy areas and techniques, and aim to upgrade general skills, such as writing (a sadly neglected skill in current academic training for economists), problem solving and understanding of government procedures.

The number of trainees each year should be limited to avoid disruption of the Commission's work but also to make it possible to reach the desired levels of competence within five years. At the end of a five-year period of implementation, the Commission should have about six Ph.D. degree holders, 20 M.Phil. degree holders and ten new M.A./M.Sc. holders.

2.4.5 Donor Intervention

The Planning Commission, as well as its predecessor ministries, has received donor assistance in capacity building since the early 1960s. Since 1990 there has been a project for assistance in capacity building in the Planning Commission that focuses on the improvement of managerial infrastructure and some computer training. The United Nations Development Programme (UNDP) and the British Government assisted in the formulation of the first Rolling Plan and Forward Budget (RPFB) and a Project Management Information System (PROMIS) designed to facilitate preparation of the RPFB. Capacity-building efforts are also being made in other areas of the Planning Commission. A number of project personnel have been trained, and some equipment purchased. However, taking a long view, repeated donor interventions have so far failed to create the required capacity.

Donor support to capacity building in the Planning Commission is mainly through short-term technical assistance from international experts. This approach has not created capacity commensurate to the resources spent. Short-term courses and workshops unrelated to any comprehensive programme for career development do not create the required level of competence and professional confidence.

2.5 THE BUREAU OF STATISTICS

The Bureau of Statistics derives its authority from, and operates under, the Statistics Ordinance of 1961. The Act compels the general public and institutions to supply data requested on principles of statistical confidentiality. The Bureau collects and processes statistics and publishes periodic reports (monthly, quarterly and annually). It also produces a number of occasional reports (census, agricultural surveys, and other special reports). The sources of the data collected by the Bureau are: the Regional Statistical Offices (with very few statisticians and limited resources); data produced by other government agencies (including the Bank of Tanzania, Customs, Line Ministries, parastatal enterprises, etc.); and periodic surveys organised by the Bureau with its own resources and/or with the support of bilateral and multilateral donors.

Improving the performance of the Bureau of Statistics is essential part of a capacity-building strategy for the Planning Commission and other economic management agencies. It is also essential to improve the quality of economic research and training in Tanzania-based universities and research institutes.

In the past the Bureau relied heavily on government agencies and public enterprises to collect economic and social data. This was adequate when government agencies, marketing boards and public monopolies controlled a high proportion of the country's economic and social life. The deregulation of the Tanzanian economy has decreased the relevance of these sources of information. The data collection and processing functions need to be redesigned in the context of proposed information strategy — revision of these methods should consider changes in the economic environment. The Bureau also needs to intensify its efforts to compare data collected by its staff with other sources of information, with a view to improving the quality and consistency of national statistics.

At this stage, the Bureau is giving a high priority to improving National Accounts, which are grossly underestimated. The review of National Accounts will indicate where gaps exist and how these gaps should be filled. Data is weak in a number of key economic and social sectors, for example: agricultural production and prices; small industrial enterprises; construction; domestic trade and transport; labour; and employment. In some cases, time and modest additional resources should suffice to exploit data that is readily available (e.g., using Customs Department data to amplify the trade accounts).

Currently, the Bureau of Statistics is a department of the Planning Commission with 48 statisticians, 129 statistical assistants, 110 supporting staff and 107 temporary staff. Most of the staff members of the Bureau need to upgrade their skills through specialised training.

TABLE 1: STATISTICAL STAFF* BY LEVEL OF EDUCATION

Education Qualifications	Male	Female	Total
Masters Degree	6	5	11
First Degree	31	6	37
Diploma	24	7	31
Certificate	22	-	22
Form VI	4	-	4
Form IV	49	14	63
Primary Education	7	2	9
Total	143	34	177

Source: Planning Commission
* Statisticians and statistical assistants

The training programme under the Swedish International Development Agency (SIDA) and other agencies has produced some qualified personnel, but more needs to be done to improve capability. It is important to increase knowledge of statistical methods, to enhance economic literacy and knowledge of national accounting conventions, to improve computer literacy, and to upgrade the 20 regional statistical offices, of which only three are currently headed by statisticians. According to an evaluation in 1994, the Bureau had sufficient equipment to perform the main function of a conventional statistical office satisfactorily. Most of the equipment has been supplied under Swedish assistance.

Basic data collection presents a problem to the Bureau of Statistics because of low response rates, absence of reliable registers to define statistical samples, inadequate means of transport and communication and the high cost of data collection. The National Master Sample (NMS) has been developed and is being accepted as the main national sample for conducting surveys in the country. It has been established that conducting surveys on the basis of the NMS improves the integrity of data collected. There is a satisfactory level of competence in sampling and survey methodology. About 50% of the total data input of the Bureau of Statistics is collected by Regional Statistical Offices (RSOs).

2.5.1 Transformation of the Bureau into an executive agency

The Bureau's administration through the Planning Commission is a source of many difficulties in recruitment, supervision and promotion of professionals and conflicts in priorities for the allocation funds. It is recommended that the Bureau should be able to operate autonomously as a government executive agency. It should diversify its products and its clients and should sell part of its output. Development of the Bureau should be linked (by the Bureau of Statistics, the Planning Commission, the Ministry of Finance, the Bank of Tanzania, universities and other concerned institutions) to the preparation of an economic information strategy that would identify the national demand for statistics and would propose programmes to meet that demand.

2.5.2 Staffing and Incentives

The Bureau does not have an appropriate incentive system to attract and retain professionals. Professionals are not compensated adequately and young graduates join the Bureau as a last resort. Proposals have been made to rationalise the functions and structure of the Bureau, and it is intended that proper job descriptions will be made, followed by determination of staffing levels. These levels will define the capacity requirements of the Bureau of Statistics in terms of training and retooling.

2.5.3 Donor Intervention

The Bureau of Statistics has enjoyed long-term donor support, including provision of necessary infrastructure, development of survey frames like the National Master sample (NMS), the Central Register of Establishments (CRE) and the development of professional and technical competencies. Other assistance is directed to strengthening the Tanzanian National Accounting System through the development of new data sources and the training of National Accounting staff. Agencies that have provided assistance include SIDA, the World Bank and UNICEF.

2.6 MINISTRY OF FINANCE

The Ministry of Finance is being restructured to increase its effectiveness. The functions of the Ministry involve the following core activities:

- formulation of overall policies for revenue collection (the operational aspects of revenue collection have been transferred to the new Tanzania Revenue Authority [TRA]);
- preparation and monitoring of Government Budget;
- mobilisation of external loans and grants as well as external debt management;
- control and reporting on government expenditures;
- monitoring and supervision of public investments;
- control and verification of government stocks/assets; and
- central payroll computerisation.

Capacity building in the Ministry of Finance will need to reflect all of the above core activities, but in terms of priorities the key areas are:

(a) budget management;
(b) external finance management;
(c) accounting systems; and
(d) government revenue management.

2.6.1 Budget Management

The management of recurrent and development budget (budget preparation, budget execution, monitoring and evaluation) is the key to any government financial management process. The Planning Commission handled the development budget process, but, in the context of ongoing reforms, the operational aspects of development budget are being transferred to the Ministry of Finance.

The Budget Department is manned by 18 professionals with academic backgrounds in finance, accountancy, economics or business administration. Most of the professionals are employed as finance management officers or accountants. Out of these 18 employees, four have Masters degrees in various fields. The rest have either B.A.s, Diplomas or Certificates in accountancy. The department is implementing a training programme supported by SIDA under the Budget Management Development Programme (BMDP). Budget skills are quite inadequate in the regions and ministries.

The budget department has embarked on a computerisation programme under BMDP. The programme aims to improve the managerial infrastructure. Through this programme, the recurrent budget has been computerised. Various computer programs are used but, because of weak co-ordination, time is wasted in converting data. The department has about 13 PCs, to be shared between 18 officers. The level of computer literacy is still low and office accommodation is grossly inadequate.

The Department staff lack appreciation of overall economic policy issues, as they have hitherto concentrated on routine budgetary matters. Skills in policy analysis must be enhanced to handle the linkage of policy and the budget. Capacity building should also include improvement in computer skills so that staff can manage the intended computerisation of the budget process. Additional computer units are needed, as each staff member should work with a computer terminal. Computerisation of the budget should be co-ordinated with that of the Accountant General's Department and of the Revenue system.

In addition to short-term training, Budget Division staff with strong potential would benefit from advanced training in public finance at the post graduate diploma or degree level. A five-year programme of two fellowships per year would provide the required capacity.

SIDA has been assisting the Budget Department since 1986, focusing on improving budget skills and provision of equipment through the Budget Management Development Programme (BMDP). The training programme covers the staff of the department and spending agencies (ministries and regions) through workshops and seminars on budget techniques and management. Training arrangements have been made in collaboration with the Institute of Development Management. The recurrent budget has been computerised and initial computer awareness has been created in the department. However, some achievement capacity still falls well short of that required to increase the effectiveness of government budgeting.

2.6.2 EXTERNAL FINANCE MANAGEMENT

Aid will remain an important element in development finance, although magnitudes are likely to decline. Given the large number of agencies involved, and the conflicting standards and requirements from the various donor aid agencies, government aid management and co-ordination is crucial. Improvements are required in the following areas: programme evaluation; financial negotiations; maintenance and analysis of data for performance, disbursement and impact evaluation; accounting and maintaining transparency in the use of aid funds; management of external debt and maintenance of data on debt profiles and servicing.

The External Finance Department has 15 members of staff with training backgrounds in finance, economics or accountancy. About 90% of the department staff are Masters degree holders employed as economists or finance management officers. Most of the departmental staff have access to computer facilities, although the level of computer literacy is insufficient.

However, despite the availability of staff with appropriate education, there are a number of deficiencies in the External Finance Department leading to weaknesses in mobilisation, allocation and efficient utilisation of external resources. Problems include the lack of coherent policies towards donor assistance, weak institutional links and co-ordination between the various parties involved on the Tanzanian side, and undeveloped negotiating skills.

External Finance Department professionals should play a vital role in mobilising and ensuring effective use of external assistance. To improve their operations, enhancement of skills is required in negotiation techniques; financial analysis; project and programme appraisal; external debt management; and computer data analysis and management.

2.6.2.1 *Donor Support*

The External Finance department has been receiving United Nations Development Programme (UNDP) capacity assistance under the Aid Management and Administration Co-ordination Systems (AMACS) Project. There are prospects for further assistance from other donor agencies in the context of a new project for Aid Management and Accountability (AMAP) to be implemented jointly by the Ministry of Finance, the Planning Commission and the Bank of Tanzania.

2.6.3 THE GOVERNMENT ACCOUNTING SYSTEM

Government accounting comes under the Accountant General in the Ministry of Finance, who has the responsibility for supervising laws, regulations, systems, accounting principles and the organisational framework for the management of public monies. In tackling these tasks, the Accountant General's Office faces a number of problems, making the standard of government accounting very poor and a source of public funds misuse. The arrangements for ensuring accountability in management and supervision of public funds are functioning poorly. There is a widespread lack of compliance with Financial Statutes and Regulations. Unrealistic budgets — with inconsistencies between planned service levels, resource requirements and resource allocations — lead to a breakdown in accountability, commitment and control. The government accounting cadre receives low remuneration, and has a poor scheme of service, low status and inadequate training. In order to improve the capacity of the Accountant Generals Department, assistance is required to:

(a) improve the working environment of the Department in the context of overall civil service reforms;
(b) improve management of the accountancy system, to develop and maintain accounting systems and improve the legislative and regulatory framework;
(c) address the specific problems of lack of expenditure control, lack of compliance and ineffective internal audit;
(d) improve the management and control of the accounting cadre;
(e) introduce an accounting code of ethics for the accounting cadre; and
(f) improve the quality of the staff and basic infrastructure.

To improve the capacity of the Accountant General's Office, it is proposed that a programme be implemented for restructuring the management and for skills development. The key components of this programme are:

- rearrangement and clarification of the responsibilities of top executives in the Department;
- development of an improved management system;
- establishment and training of a Systems Development Unit;
- improvements to the centralised payment and expenditure control system; and
- establishment of a Regional Sub-Treasury system to replace the Regional Accounting Units.

A programme also needs to be implemented to improve the morale, motivation and productivity of the accounting cadre through:

- allocating clear responsibilities to all accounting staff;
- improving knowledge about the accounting cadre (numbers, levels, location, performance, qualifications, skills etc.);
- improving recruitment methods;
- performance reviews;
- promotion, transfer and discipline enforcement; and
- implementing a comprehensive training scheme.

An immediate requirement is the exposure of Accounting Department senior executives to practices in other countries, and modern methods and facilities.

2.6.3.1 *Training*

In total, as of June 1996, there are 2860 accountants and auditors registered in the books of the Registrar of the National Board of Accountants and Auditors (NBAA), working in both public and private sectors. The central government has about 2080 accounting staff in its workforce, though not all are registered with the NBAA. The number of accounting staff employed by local government could not be established, but it is understood that there is a deficiency of accounting personnel, particularly in remote district councils. As a result, non-accounting staff perform some of the accounting functions.

Most of the central government accounting staff have professional qualifications ranging from basic accounting certificates to ACCA (Association of Certified Chartered Accountants) or CPA(T) (Certified Public Accountant [Tanzania]). The number of highest qualified accounting staff (CPA or ACCA) working with the central government is very small. However, current training needs mainly relate to improving management and supervision skills, acquiring new concepts and methods and learning from the experience of others. Table 2, below, shows the type of training required.

TABLE 2: ACCOUNTANT GENERAL DEPARTMENT: STAFF DEVELOPMENT PROGRAMME 1995/96 - 1997/98

CATEGORY OF TRAINING	ANNUAL TARGET			TOTAL CANDIDATES	COURSE DURATION	COURSE OBJECTIVES
	1995/96	1996/97	1997/98			
Management training for top executives	10	10	10	30	3-4 weeks	To equip them with deeper insight of their responsibilities and latest techniques of finance
Management training for Senior Officers	20	20	20	60	1-2 months	To enable senior officers acquire analytical tools for modern financial accounting and control.
Middle level officers	20	20	20	60	3-6 months	To improve competence
Undergraduate studies in accounting finance	40	40	40	60	3-6 months	To acquire knowledge and skills in financial accounting practices
Training for professional level or ordinary level diploma	20	20	20	60	12 months	To provide professional training in accounting
(a) Training for ATEC II (b) Training for ATEC I	15 15	15 15	15 15	45 45	12 months 13 months	To provide training to middle level posts and technicians
Information technology and Computer application	30	30	30	90	3 weeks	To equip professionals with computer knowledge
	170	170	170	510		

2.7 TANZANIA REVENUE AUTHORITY (TRA)

In August 1995, the Government established the Tanzania Revenue Authority (TRA) as an independent body responsible for, inter alia, administering revenue laws and assessing, collecting and accounting for those revenues. The authority is an executive agency of the government, and operates outside the civil service framework to allow for operational flexibility. The establishment of TRA followed a long experience of inadequate collection of tax revenue due to weak administrative arrangements, corruption and evasion, as well as poor working conditions and facilities for tax personnel.

The workforce of the previous tax department was poorly motivated, had very poor working conditions and systems and bad management, and there were high incidences of corruptive practices. For many years, the Revenue Departments remained ill-equipped in terms of office accommodation, transport, working equipment and staff housing. The Revenue Departments also operated with very poor tax assessment and collection systems, which were open for abuse and incapable of producing quality results.

In view of the poor structure and conditions the TRA inherited from the previous system, capacity building is needed in several main areas:

(a) The Government has allocated to TRA the office buildings of the defunct Tanzania Housing Bank, but they are not in good condition. Countrywide rehabilitation, replacements and refurbishment of offices will be necessary in order to create the basic environment for effectiveness and efficiency.

(b) After undertaking job-description and manning-level assessment, it will be important to carry out training at all levels. Tax administration is not a field for which people can be drawn from the open market without special training. The Institute of Tax Administration (ITA) requires substantial improvements in trainer capabilities, as well as course coverage and levels, and training facilities. While ITA is being improved, the shortfall in trained personnel should be alleviated by short-term courses conducted by local and foreign trainers, particularly in the areas of investigation, management, computer application and the training of trainers. Also, short-term overseas training for senior managers will be needed.

(c) The effectiveness of revenue collection is constrained by continued dependence on outdated manual systems, making the processing, storage and retrieval of data difficult. Assistance is required to determine the most appropriate computerisation system, in light of the ongoing efforts to introduce the Automated System of Customs Data Management, the Value Added Tax System for the Sales Tax and Inland Revenue Department, and computerisation efforts of the Income Tax Department.

At this stage TRA has approached several donors for support, and commitments have been received from the World Bank, USAID and ODA for partial coverage of the above requirements.

2.8 THE EXCHEQUER AND AUDIT DEPARTMENT

The Exchequer and Audit Department is an independent department of government established by an Act of Parliament. The main functions of the department are: to ensure that withdrawals or exchequer issues from the consolidated funds services are made according to parliamentary approval; to audit accounts for all offices of government; and to prepare and submit annual audit reports to the President for tabling before Parliament.

The audit report produced by the Controller and Auditor General is an important tool for management of government finances. The timely production of quality reports is critical for economic and financial management.

The department employs about 352 managerial and technical staff. Most of them are of the accounting profession. However, the number of fully qualified auditors in external audit is very small. The majority of staff have technician level qualifications. Most audit staff have received little or no training other than courses for the professional examinations for the NBAA. Out of the 352 managerial and technical staff, only one has acquired Masters level in accounting, four have Bachelor of Commerce degrees and 48 have diplomas. 299 are educated to either Form IV or VI school-leavers' level.

Training institutions for audit staff include the Institute of Development Management (IDM Mzumbe), the Institute of Finance Management (IFM), and the Dar es Salaam and Arusha Schools of Accountancy.

The Ex-Audit Department has embarked on a computerisation programme. The Department has been provided with nine computer units under a World Bank loan. A few officers have received training in computer application. In view of weaknesses in the Audit Department, capacity building is required in the form of:

(a) improved audit training for the technical staff in the lower levels, and managerial training for the senior officers;
(b) improvement in the supply of computer facilities, in addition to units provided by the World Bank, which serve the Head Office only. For efficient auditing and reporting, regional and ministerial offices have to be equipped as well;
(c) training in computer skills; and
(d) training in performance auditing.

Two donors — the Department for International Development (DFID) (formerly Oversesas Development Administration [ODA]) and the World Bank — are assisting the Ex-Audit Department in the areas of training and provision of logistical support. However, it should be noted that the effectiveness of the auditing system is far from being simply a matter of technique. Despite the constraints facing it, the Auditor General's Department has been able, from time to time, to expose serious cases of financial misconduct and poor performance, but often there has been a lack of political will to act on the findings. In auditing, as well as in other aspects of financial capacity, improved technical capacity will only result in improved financial performance if backed up by the political will to impose financial discipline and to punish wrong-doing.

2.9 LAND MANAGEMENT

Land management is central to any sustainable economic development, especially where the private sector is called upon to provide a lead input for economic growth. In Tanzania, potential investors have been constrained by uncertainties and delays associated with land and services allocations. Surveyed land is in seriously short supply and, even where available, procedures to gain access to land are non-transparent. Areas calling for capacity assistance include:

a) Urban Land Policy: There is a need for a land policy that makes more economic sense. Government revenues should benefit from the allocation of scarce lands, rather than allowing windfall benefits to accrue to officials and those lucky enough to gain access. There is a need for resource mobilisation from forms of income generation from within the sub-sector;
b) Land Survey: To allow faster survey of land and a more flexible adjustment of land use controls to the needs of the growing economy; and
c) Land Services: For easier and faster access and use by development agencies and industrialists (water, power, roads, etc.) and for settlements in a competitive business environment.

2.10 CONCLUSIONS

The Planning Commission faces new challenges as a result of the shift from a command- to a market-based economy. The Commission is now required to put more emphasis on economic analysis, trouble-shooting and policy work, as opposed to investment planning and control. However, the quality of economic analysis performed by the Planning Commission is constrained by the low capacity of the Bureau of Statistics, by a poor working environment (including office space) and inadequate staff management and development policies. The Planning Commission workforce needs reorientation to the new needs of the environment of an open and competitive economy in which the private sector assumes increasing responsibilities. The coverage, reliability and precision of economic statistics in Tanzania must be improved. The Bureau of Statistics needs to be strengthened and should operate as an executive agency to enhance flexibility and diversify its activities and facilitate co-operation with the private sector, which is now its a main source of statistics. The Bureau of Statistics staff should receive further training and be provided with adequate logistical support and an attractive scheme of service.

The Ministry of Finance is being restructured. Substantial capacity-building initiatives are needed in the areas of budget management, external finance, accounting and government revenue management. Serious deficiencies in terms of staff numbers and logistical support have to be addressed in these key areas.

The Tanzania Revenue Authority (TRA) — which was established to administer the revenue laws and to assess, collect and account for revenue — should be strengthened by training, and improved equipment and working environment. The Controller and Auditor General's Department is another area which calls for urgent strengthening. In order to accelerate the promotion of private sector investments, land planning and survey and associated land policies are also critical areas for capacity building.

3. CAPACITY OF THE CIVIL SERVICE IN TANZANIA: AN ASSESSMENT

3.1 INTRODUCTION

The civil service is the operational arm of government charged with analysis, formulation, and administration of public policy. Its institutions include ministries, autonomous departments and commissions at the centre, a well as regional and district administration and local government.

The capacity of the civil service can be defined in terms of its ability as an institution (or a set of organisational units) to perform functions effectively, efficiently and sustainably. Capacity is a continuing process — it is not a passive state. The civil service is a set of organisations structured so that individuals interact in their endeavour to attain common objectives; and the utilisation of potential capacity of individuals is the key to the effective operation of the institution. The retention of existing capacity, the improvement in utilisation of existing capacity and the retrieval of capacity that has been eroded are important as efforts to create new capacity.

Thus the capacity of the civil service is defined in a broad sense as encompassing not only human resource development but also the institutional framework, pay and terms of service, work culture, administrative and office technologies and working conditions. Capacity development is not solely a matter of hiring and training staff, but requires having in place within the service an environment in which skilled people are utilised effectively, are retained within the service and are motivated to best perform their tasks.

3.2 OVERALL CONTEXT OF CIVIL SERVICE CAPACITY

Economic environment and the role of the government

The civil service in Tanzania is facing tremendous challenges. Public administration is characterised by inefficiency, poorly paid and unmotivated employees, widespread corruption and a low level of service delivery. The poor economic situation constitutes both an important cause and a result of weak administration. Improved functioning of the civil service is one prerequisite for the development of a sound private sector economy.

Since the mid-1980s Tanzania has been implementing macroeconomic reforms based on agreements with the IMF and the World Bank. The reforms resulted in a transition towards a more market-oriented economy. This requires a change in economic management from a regime of direct controls to one eliciting response indirectly through various policy and incentive instruments. The government is thus changing its role from commanding to steering the economy in which it seeks to play a catalytic, facilitating role. There is an ongoing transfer of responsibilities to produce goods and services from government departments and parastatals to private corporate bodies and individuals. But this process does not mean that the need for effective government has diminished. The government needs an efficient, professional, committed civil service force to supply public services and manage policies to support the private sector participation in the economy. There is a need for new skills; the civil service needs to learn new ways of functioning, to adopt a new work culture and generally acquire new set of core competencies.

Political Environment

With political liberalisation and democratisation, various groups in society have greater freedom to articulate their views of public policies. This has been accentuated by the significant increase in freedom of the press, with greater media involvement in probing the management of public affairs enhancing public awareness and facilitating public scrutiny of government performance. Thus, the civil service must address the challenge of enhancing the ability of government to respond to the needs of the public, and at the same time to encourage the various actors in the economy to adjust their behaviour in the broader context of interests of society.

The Tanzanian political leadership has been committed, in principle, to capacity development of the civil service, but their actions have not always been consistent with the achievement of that objective. Immediately after Independence in 1961, there was a reasonable level of professionalism in the civil service. The policies of localisation and later those of self sufficiency in manpower by the year 1980 were all geared to ensuring that the public service would be staffed by sufficient qualified people in all spheres. The number of trained staff increased considerably. However, with the extension of the role of the State, and the need to staff the large number of parastatals created following 1967, available professionals were spread thinly over a wide range of tasks. Moreover, commitment to an egalitarian incomes policy combined with the effects of inflation to erode the real incomes of professionals.

Brain drain

Although there has been no study of the international brain drain from Tanzania, there is casual evidence that many professional Tanzanians migrated to find better paying jobs in other countries in Africa, especially in Central and Southern Africa, as well as overseas. Internal mobility, particularly to the parastatals, also depleted the civil service.

The labour market

Until recently the labour market, especially for higher level skills, was monopolised by the government. All graduates from institutions of higher learning were, on graduation, allocated jobs by the National Higher Level Manpower Allocation Committee (NHLMAC), based on the preferences they indicated. In effect, this meant that throughout most of the period since Independence, there was no competition for entry to civil service, and no process of élite selection; any graduate could expect employment, and the best would aspire to employment in the parastatals. One potentially positive aspect of recent developments is the development of much more competition among graduates for scarce jobs, carrying with it the possibility of recruitment to the civil service being placed on a more competitive, meritocratic footing.

Impact of HIV/AIDS

The first three AIDS cases in Tanzania were reported in 1983. The National AIDS Control Programme (NACP) estimated that, by December 1992, about 800,000 people (3.2% of the population) were infected with the disease, i.e., were HIV sero-positive. Of these, approximately 120,000 had already developed AIDS, i.e., crossed the threshold from being infected to being ill. The remainder would develop AIDS sometime between less than one and up to ten years from the date of infection. AIDS is now believed to have surpassed malaria as the leading killer disease among adults, and is likely to do so for children in the very near future.

There are wide disparities across different subgroups of the population, HIV infection levels are highest in people between the ages of 15 and 45 and in new-born infants. However, HIV infection rates are increasing rapidly, especially among adolescents. Although women and men are about equally infected, on average women appear to become infected at a younger age than men. The highest rates of infection are for 30-39 year old men and in 25-29 year old women.

The virus is claiming the lives of some of the most qualified and skilled people in the civil service. There is great need to reduce the rate of transmission of HIV, not only for the general development of Tanzania but also for the protection of the country's trained human resources.

3.3 EXISTING CAPACITY, PROBLEMS AND CONSTRAINTS OF HUMAN RESOURCES IN THE CIVIL SERVICE

The civil service in Tanzania has expanded greatly over the years, from 89,745 employees in 1961 to 315,963 employees in 1994, as illustrated in Table 3 below.

TABLE 3: GROWTH IN CIVIL SERVICE EMPLOYMENT: 1961-1994

Sector	FY 61	FY 65	FY 71	FY 75	FY 81	FY 85	FY 88	FY 93	FY 94
Education	11,145	14,215	23,131	32,735	93,318	95,551	101,042	128,410	n.a
Health	6,300	10,000	12,400	13,00	17,036	30,193	32,650	37,705	n.a
Other	72,300	647,05	103,072	102,488	104,745	135,062	165,446	190,497	n.a
Total	89,745	89,847	138,60	148,228	215,099	260,806	299,138	354,612	315,963

Source: Civil Service Reform Programme

The civil service census of 1988 revealed that the civil service consists of few professionals and administrators and many middle-level technicians and lower-level staff as indicated in Table 4 below. Of the 300,000-plus civil servants, 60% had an educational level of up to primary school only (see Table 5). It was further revealed that 44% of civil servants were assigned duties for which they had no relevant skills and that 51% of all civil servants with supervisory and administrative responsibilities at various levels did not possess the required supervisory and administrative skills (see Table 6).

TABLE 4: DISTRIBUTION OF GOVERNMENT EMPLOYEES ACCORDING TO MAJOR OCCUPATION GROUPS

MAIN OCCUPATIONS	EMPLOYEES	%
Administrators/legislators	5,552	1.84
Professionals	11,791	3.9
Technicians and Associate Professionals	187,317	62.05
Clerks	14,359	4.76
Service Workers	40,394	13.38
Craft/Related Workers	280	0.09
Plant and Machine Operators	7,821	2.59
Elementary Occupations	34,108	11.30

Source: CSRP

3.3.1 *Training*

The quality of civil servants' training has an impact on their capacity to carry out their duties. Induction training that is task specific and clearly linked to inculcating the organisational culture is no longer undertaken in the civil service. Staff development has not been emphasised in the personnel management practices of government. Any training that takes place through training programmes, workshops or seminars is not related to specific goals of performance improvement. Training is unsystematic and poorly programmed, so that a few individuals can attend a number of programmes consecutively while many others do not attend a single programme in their entire working lives.

TABLE 5: DISTRIBUTION OF EMPLOYEES IN FUNCTIONAL GROUPS ACCORDING TO HIGHEST LEVEL OF FORMAL EDUCATION (TANZANIA)

	HIGHEST LEVEL OF EDUCATION						
	GRADUATE AND POST GRADUATE	COLLEGE	SECONDARY	ELEMENTARY	BELOW ELEME-NTARY	NOT STATED	BELOW
OPERATIONAL SERVICE	23 0.04%	610 0.95%	1898 2.96%	57019 89.03%	4462 6.97%	34 0.05%	64046
JUNIOR SUPPORT	6 0.02%	943 2.80%	8083 24.00%	23880 0.91%	730 2.17%	34 0.10%	33676
MIDDLE SUPPORT	261 0.18	5232 3.51%	41212 27.66%	100879 67.70%	1087 0.73	335 0.22%	149006
MIDDLE MANAGEMENT	6035 11.33	3179 5.97%	29135 54.69%	14293 26.83%	485 0.91	146 0.27%	53273
SENIOR MANAGEMENT	705 56.04%	85 6.76%	408 32.43%	49 3.90%	7 0.56%	4 0.32%	1258
SENIOR MANAGEMENT ADMIN	426 79.48%	11 14.55%	78 1.49%	8 1.49%	8 0.93%	5 0.93%	536
Not Stated	1 1.61%	1 1.61%	21 33.87%	32 51.61%	5 8.06%	2 3.23%	62
TOTAL NUMBER % this represents	7457 2.47%	10061 3.33%	80835 26.78%	196160 64.98%	6784 2.25%	560 0.19%	301857

TABLE 6: DISTRIBUTION OF EMPLOYEES IN PROFESSIONAL AND TECHNICAL/ASSOCIATED PROFESSIONAL RELATED JOBS WITH INADEQUATE SKILLS, TANZANIA

	PROFESSIONAL			TECHNICIANS/ASSOCIATE PROFESSIONALS			
	Inadequate Skills			Inadequate Skills			Overall Total
FUNCTIONAL GROUP	Total	Number	Percent	Total	Number	Percent	
Senior Management and Administrative	725	166	23	762	45	6	1,794
Senior Management	6,999	3,398	48	42,259	12,831	3[illegible]	53,273
Middle Support	3,996	3,328	95	1	69,855	78	148,723
Operational Service and Junior Support	244	288	93	42,939	3,725	87	
Total	11,964	7,664	64	187,295	86,456	46	301443

Source: CSRP

As a result of the cumulative impact of weak personnel development, constraints in human resources in the civil service include the following.

(a) Inadequate managerial and technical skills — there is a general weakness in management in the public sector. Where good management exists, it can be credited to innate leadership qualities and instincts rather than to training. Failure to transact government business as a result of lack of management skills is reflected in many areas.

(b) Weak training co-ordination and low training capacity — the current institutional framework for co-ordination of civil service training is too centralised, ad hoc, bureaucratic and irregular. Although the Civil Service Department is supposed to co-ordinate and give guidance (Staff Circular No.3 of 1967) it has failed to do so because of lack of resources and capacity. As a result, there is lack of a civil service training strategy, proliferation of training institutions, and failure to utilise training fellowship effectively. The civil service internal training capacity is very low, as existing training institutions cater for lower level occupations — clerks, office managers, typists, accounts assistants and tax officers. Senior staff have to learn on the job in a weak institutional setting.

(c) Supply-driven, classroom-oriented and individual-based training — classroom training away from the workplace is emphasised, based on the availability of course offers. It is individual based and not task oriented. It is not integrated into the personnel management system nor related to organised staff development efforts. The civil service lacks a system for training prioritisation, identification of training needs and selection of employees to be trained.

(d) Low training management capacity — training officers allocated to Ministries lack training management skills. There is an absence of overall guidance in terms of training manuals, training information systems and training needs identification and programming systems. The Civil Service Department, the Civil Service Commission and Ministries also lack training equipment.

(e) The gender factor — women civil servants continue to be inhibited by historical and cultural prejudices, yet there are no deliberate programmes aimed at changing prejudices, or remedial interventions and empowerment programmes aimed at raising women's participation in training programmes.

(f) Lack of concern for other special groups including the disabled and the gifted. People with disabilities, particularly those who are disabled while in civil service employment, are not catered for. There are no identification mechanisms or special training programmes for the gifted.

3.3.2 Utilisation of Human Resources

There are widespread problems of utilisation of human resources within the civil service caused principally by poor incentive systems. There is also poor deployment of human resources within the service, as is exemplified in the deployment of primary school teachers. Many rural districts have very high pupil-teacher ratios, while the major urban centres, especially Dar es Salaam, have low pupil-teacher ratios (i.e., they are relatively over-staffed). Similar patterns are also easily observed in cadres serving in other rural services, such as health and agriculture. This imbalance in staffing between different areas of the country legitimises low productivity in some places while denying services to others. Likewise, transfers among different civil service groups do take place frequently and unsystematically.

3.4. CIVIL SERVICE: ORGANISATION AND MANAGEMENT PRACTICES

3.4.1 Structure and Status

The Civil Service Act of 1962 envisaged a 'proper' civil service to comprise 'permanent and pensionable' government employees appointed by the Civil Service Commission (CSC). Subsequent policy and political measures, which were ultimately embodied in the 1989 Civil Service Act, effectively removed the criteria of the 'permanent and pensionable' status and appointment by the CSC from the definition of a civil servant. Over the years, the government has admitted significant numbers of appointments (at salary grade GS2 and below) into permanent and pensionable status and today, in virtually all administrative aspects, there is no distinction between civil servants and local government employees.

The loss of control of employment and decline in professionalism in the Tanzania civil service coincided with the abandonment of the distinction between the career civil service cadre of permanent and pensionable employees, and the operational service non-pensionable cadre. The massive but unsuccessful 1972 initiative to decentralise public administration, accompanied by the scrapping of local governments, resulted in the over-expansion of the civil service establishment.

A career civil service should be characterised by recruitment and promotion based on merit, a decent remuneration backed by a pension, no involvement in business, and security of tenure. Until the 1970s the permanent and pensionable status in government employment was reserved for a relatively small and stable cadre and entry into the cadre was controlled.

3.4.2 Fragmentation of Policy and Management Institutions

The institutional framework for the management of government employment is fragmented. Appointments into government employment are carried out by:

- local authorities for all cadres of staff below staff grade GS4 (i.e., including OS grades) within technical departments;
- the Local Government Service Commission (LGSC) for grades GS5 to GS9 deployed in the local authorities;
- the Minister for Local Government for Heads of Departments in some councils;
- the 'Kamati za Ajira Serikalini' (KAMUS) for grades GS2 and below;
- the Teachers Service Commission (TSC) for all teachers;
- the Civil Service Commission (CSC) for grades GS3 to GS8; and
- the President for GS9-GS10 and for all super scale/director/heads of department grades in both the civil and local government services.

In the case of professional and technical staff deployed into local authorities, there is a multitude of employers — various Ministries that are in charge of respective schemes of service, committees of councillors, LGSC, CSC, the MOLG, and the President).

3.4.3 Breakdown of Authority and Accountability Regimes

Authority and accountability broke down at two levels. First, there was an initiative to politicise the civil service under the one-party socialist regime. Whatever its merits, one unfortunate consequence of this initiative was that it undermined the historical authority and accountability structures. Party and trade union cadres gained influence at the expense of civil service managers. Those in authority started to shy away from exercising it and thereby contributed to erosion of discipline and accountability.

Second, there was a breakdown in the accountability regimes because of weaknesses in the personnel management and performance appraisal mechanisms. Many government officers have neither clearly defined job descriptions nor work targets, leaving little possibility for performance appraisal.

3.4.4 THE CIVIL SERVICE PAY AND INCENTIVE SYSTEM

At Independence, and for a decade thereafter, Tanzania was able to pay its civil servants meaningful salaries, but subsequent years saw a severe deterioration in civil service pay. In the decade of mid-1970s to mid-1980s there was a precipitate drop in the real value of civil service salaries. Even earlier, the real levels of compensation for senior civil servants had deteriorated as a result of a deliberate pursuit of egalitarian goals. By 1984 civil service salaries were on average, in real terms, only about 31% of their 1969 levels, but the top salary level was considerably worse, at 11% (see Table 7 below).

TABLE 7: FALL IN REAL WAGE FOR CIVIL SERVICE EMPLOYEES (1969-1984)

Year	Minimum Salary (T.shs./month)	Average Salary (T.shs./month)	Top Salary (T.shs./month)
1969	100	100	100
1974	135	133	56
1979	58	77	26
1984	40	31	11

Source: CSRP

In spite of the economic recovery in the latter half of the 1980s, the decline in the real levels of civil service salaries persisted, with civil service salaries in real terms generally remaining depressed below FY1984/85 levels. However, there have been significant rises in basic salaries in the past two years. Still, the minimum basic salary level in real terms is estimated at less than one quarter of what it was in the late 1960s (see Table 8 below). Civil servants are comparatively disadvantaged in relation to their colleagues in parastatals. Currently, the government is unable to pay civil servants a minimum living wage. There is little incentive to improve work performance and little willingness to accept greater responsibility.

TABLE 8: MINIMUM AND TOP CIVIL SERVICE BASIC SALARIES IN REAL TERMS (1976 PRICES), 1984/85-1995/96

Year	Minimum wage (T.shs./month) 1976 Prices	Top Salaries (T.shs./month) 1976 Prices
1984/85	238	n/a
1985/86	236	n/a
1986/87	223	n/a
1987/88	180	1,074
1988/89	158	865
1989/90	176	1,574
1990/91	182	1,670
1991/92	189	1,423
1992/93	219	1,157
1993/94	180	1,091
1994/95	282	n/a
1995/96	391	n/a

Source: CSRP

Non-salary allowances and in-kind benefits significantly mitigated both the low basic salaries and the compression of the civil service salary structure. However, this has had the negative consequence of rendering the compensation systems non-transparent, inequitable, and difficult to manage. Furthermore, the distorted compensation structure exacerbated the government's fiscal problems, because the wage bill could not be either reliably budgeted or controlled.

3.4.5 Personnel Management Practices

3.4.5.1 *Recruitment and Selection*

Current recruitment procedures are not based on competence, merit or demonstrated ability of individuals, resulting in the recruitment of some incompetent and under-qualified individuals employed on 'permanent and pensionable' terms. Entrance is not subject to qualifications or an entry examination. Graduates from training institutions have been allocated to the civil service regardless of their personal suitability, enthusiasm or commitment.

Organisations are most likely to recruit talent using open public announcements to solicit applications, rigorous examinations or interviews to determine entry, with an independent review board to set recruitment criteria and ensure objectivity. As a result of the supply driven central allocation mechanisms, the government has accumulated some staff who should not be in the service. Appointments have been based on informal contacts rather than established procedures, limiting the likelihood of appointing the best qualified people into job positions, and limiting the possibilities of identifying and locating the most competent personnel.

3.4.5.2 *Promotions and Career Advancement*

In many cases, promotions are given to individuals with poor work records, while those who perform well are left behind. The way promotions have been carried out in government has acted as a disincentive and a source of discouragement for the staff, who see their less competent peers moving up the career ladder while they are left behind.

Weaknesses in promotion and career development can be traced to a poor work-assessment system as well as poor leadership skills. Staff assessment exercises have emphasised personal relationships rather than work performance and output. On the other hand, the leadership that determines who is to be promoted has not been committed enough to institutional development and systematic approaches to staff development.

3.4.5.3 *Work Motivation, Work Supervision and Discipline*

Apart from low pay and poor levels of remuneration, the general application of morale-boosting methods is totally lacking in the government employment system. Appreciation and encouragement from immediate supervisors is lacking. There is a general weakness in work supervision, as well as laxity in applying disciplinary measures where necessary. As a result, poor discipline at work characterises all sections of government employment.

3.4.6 ADMINISTRATIVE TECHNOLOGIES

The availability of office equipment, office machines and office furniture is generally inadequate. Most equipment is obsolete and there is no standardisation in equipping government offices. While offices with technical assistance are better equipped with word processors and photocopiers, other offices still use old manual typewriters and manual duplicating machines. Internal communication within Ministries and between Ministries and the general public is a major headache. Maintenance 'culture' in many offices is lacking. There is little preventative maintenance, and often, although equipment is in place, it may not be in working condition.

The Ministry of Finance and the Civil Service Department are mainly responsible for formulating policies on administrative technologies for the civil service. While the Treasury is concerned with the financial aspect, the Civil Service Department is responsible for approving all purchases of administrative technologies. The Civil Service Department is also responsible for keeping abreast of technological development. However, no research on new technologies is carried out, and there is no government office technology policy.

3.5 POSSIBLE RESPONSES TO PROBLEMS AND CONSTRAINTS

3.5.1 THE CIVIL SERVICE REFORM PROGRAMME: VISION, OBJECTIVES AND STRATEGY

On the basis of a capacity assessment of the civil service, the government has packed a range of options into the Civil Service Reform Programme (CSRP). The vision is a new civil service guided by the realisation that the rigid bureaucracies of the past cannot cope with rapidly changing technology. There is a need to transform the civil service from a command and control bureaucratic culture into a more decentralised, flexible, innovative and entrepreneurial style. It is envisaged that the future civil service will be characterised by:

(a) professionalism;
(b) impartiality and objectivity in decision making;
(c) integrity;
(d) anonymity of legitimately-made decisions;
(e) being non-partisan/apolitical, but loyal to the government of the day; and
(f) transparency and accountability in decisions and actions.

The cornerstones of a professional, politically impartial, disciplined, efficient and effective civil service will be based on:

- the recruitment of civil servants on the basis of open and fair competition;
- promotion of staff on the basis of merit;
- competitive remuneration of civil servants; and
- security of tenure for those civil servants who demonstrate integrity, discipline and good performance.

The Government's fundamental goal in launching the CSRP is to achieve a smaller, affordable, well-compensated, efficient and effectively-performing civil service. In this context, the Government also seeks to transform the civil service in its role, functions and structures, and to improve its skills and capacity so that these are relevant and consistent with the redefined policies for national economic development and delivery of public services, involving a greatly enhanced role for the private sector. Further, in this vision, the Government will pursue the decentralisation of its functions by strengthening local government institutions. The reform seeks to ensure that the civil service provides the public with value for money. However, realisation of these objectives will only be possible through relatively lengthy and complex processes.

The key features of this programme comprise:

(a) reducing the role and functions of the government — not just by divesting but by systematically exploring alternative mechanisms for delivery of services;
(b) improving the quality, motivation, morale and performance of civil servants;
(c) decentralising functions and services delivery to local government councils, autonomous and self-financing government agencies, NGOs and community-based organisations; and
(d) contracting out non-core and auxiliary services to efficient private sector operators.

3.5.2 CAPACITY BUILDING

Capacity building is a central component of the Civil Service Reform Programme. The issue of pay reform appears critical to the CSRP undertaking, but is a difficult issue in the light of the public wage bill ceilings that are part of the economic stabilisation programme. As a start, the Government has put in place a rationalised pay structure for the civil service, in which all allowances have been consolidated into the salary scales. However, this has not resulted in any decompression of the net pay structure.

A government service employment policy is currently being prepared. Open and competitive recruitment and promotion, and the performance appraisal system, are being reviewed. The Civil Service Commission is to be reformed to make it an effective tool for overseeing merit-based recruitment and personnel management systems. To promote commitment and professional behaviour, a code of ethics for the top leadership is already in place, and a similar code for the rest of the civil servants is being prepared.

Organisation and efficiency reviews have been completed in the Central Ministries and in the Economic and Social Sector Ministries. Phase Two implementation of the Organisation and Efficiency Reforms has started in the four Central Ministries. Others are due to begin soon.

3.6 CONCLUSION

Although the Government is implementing reforms, Ministries still lack the requisite skills to carry out their functions. In terms of capacity, what is required is something akin to a cultural transformation — a change in the attitudes, values and modes of administrative behaviour cultivated over a period of nearly 30 years. The Civil Service Reform Programme has developed a vision of a reformed civil service, but the success of the reforms depends on effective implementation of management practices that will change the way the system works.

Important issues that must be confronted include:

- the urgent need to upgrade the general level of skills within the civil service through a sustained programme of staff development;
- the need for the government to strive to pay its key employees a competitive wage; and
- the need to explore further how civil service capacity can be enhanced, given the limited resources.

4. LOCAL AND REGIONAL ADMINISTRATION IN TANZANIA

4.1 Regional Administration

Regional administrations are made up of central government (civil) servants occupying regional and district offices. Their functions, as set out in Act No. 12 of 1982, cover areas of education, health, agriculture, natural resources, water, land development, community development and works. Their responsibilities centre around interpretation of government policy and playing a co-ordinative role between central government ministries and local authorities. Functions performed by them through the Regional Development Committee as stipulated under Section 10 of Act No.12 of 1982 include:

(a) providing advice to local government authorities regarding their development plans and support for projects or programmes of a local government authority;
(b) providing advice to the government regarding ministerial development projects, programmes and activities affecting or relating to the region; and
(c) promotion and supervision of government plans and programmes within the region.

This requires regional staff to comprehend and interpret policies, understand the scope of their responsibilities and to have the capacity to guide local governments.

4.2 LOCAL ADMINISTRATION

The local authorities are made up of councils of elected representative plus a team of public servants under an Executive Director. The relationship between the two components of the local government authorities is critical to its functioning, as is the relationship with the central government. Local authorities are responsible for the provision of such services as primary education, primary health care, district roads, water supplies, etc. They are responsible for the maintenance of peace, order and good government, and the promotion of social welfare and economic well being in their area of jurisdiction. Subject to national policy and plans for rural and urban development, they are supposed to further social and economic development.

4.3 EXISTING LEVEL OF CAPACITY

4.3.1 LOCAL GOVERNMENT

4.3.1.1 *Councils*

The highest policy decision-making body in a district is the district council. It is made up mainly of members elected one from each ward in the area of the district council, Members of Parliament representing constituents within the area of the district council in the Assembly, national Members of Parliament resident in the district and other members elected by the district council, including one from among the chairpersons of village councils within the area of the district councils.

Councillors should be citizens of the United Republic of Tanzania, at least 21 years of age and not employed by the authority. The criteria of eligibility for election disregard levels of education (except basic literacy) as well as property status of the candidates. There has been wide variability in the level and quality of participation of the elected representatives, with significant differences in the level of understanding of their role in the affairs of their respective local authorities. Councillors have tended to interfere with day-to-day operations of the authorities usurping the role of the executive, thereby undermining their own policymaking and control functions. There have been other instances when elected representatives have become servile to the executive arm of the local government authority in order to earn its favours, including pecuniary benefits.

The head of the executive arm is the executive director, who is both secretary to the district council and the leader of a district management team comprising department heads at that level and other senior officers.

Under the Local Government Service Act, 1982, district authorities have little say over the appointment of a large number of their officers. The maintenance and control of the local government service was by and large vested in the Local Government Service Commission. The President appoints the Chairman of the Commission, and the Minister responsible for local government appoints its members. The Minister is further empowered to formulate a scheme for the establishment of a local government service, which must be confirmed by the National Assembly.

The Local Government Service Scheme — which is the basis for the 'promotion, development, maintenance and control of an efficient local government service' — gives the President enormous powers over the administration of local government. In this connection, the President can direct:

> *...that the power of making appointments to certain offices in the service of local government authorities to which the scheme applies, and of transfer, promotion or appointment, dismissal and disciplinary control of certain persons appointed to any such offices shall be exercised by such person or body of persons as he may direct.*

> *He may direct that certain functions and duties...be exercised or discharged by the Minister, the Commission, its members or officers or by the local government authorities to which the scheme applies, their members and officers or by members of the Service or persons in the service of the Government ...* (Act No 10,1982).

The Act further empowers the President to delegate his considerable powers to any body or person(s). The President delegates the constitution of offices and appointments in the local government to the Local Government Service Commission subject to approval by the Minister responsible for local government.

The Act states that 'a local government authority may appoint to its service such officers and other staff, to whom the Scheme does not apply...' and that no local government authority is allowed to appoint or dismiss an officer or employee whose monthly emoluments exceed such sum as the Commission may specify for the local government officer. This, in effect, means that local government authorities are barred from employing any professional staff since all employees in Salary Scale GS2 and above are subject to the Local Government Service Scheme administered by the Local Government Service Commission.

Admittedly, the Act empowers a local government authority to interdict any of its officers or employees but this is subject to 'prior approval of the proper office', and even then it has no power to remove such officers or employees from office. This responsibility is reserved for the appointing authority — either the President, or the Minister, or the Local Government Service Commission. This has resulted in widespread criticism and complaints from the local government authorities. It is argued that the Commission has abused its powers under this provision and that gross misconduct and embezzlement have either been handsomely rewarded through promotion of the culprits or mildly punished through a transfer from one authority to another. An April 1992 amendment to the local Government Service Act took away some of the powers of the Local Government Service Commission, but left it with the power to employ officers (other than the Heads of Departments and Executive Directors in the district and urban authorities, who are appointed by the Minister, and for municipalities and city council by the President). The amendment provided for a disciplinary committee at the local authority level, which can only make recommendations to the disciplinary authority of the appointing authority.

One argument put forward for these arrangements, which deny local government authorities the right to hire and fire their officers, is that they rely on central government subventions for at least 80% of their recurrent expenditures and for 100% of development programmes. One challenge is for local governments to develop the capacity to collect revenue. Current estimates suggest that urban authorities collect barely 10% of potentially collectable revenues from property and market levies.

The situation is less clear cut for district authorities, because of their narrower revenue bases, limited to produce cess and poll tax (development levy). Many of these revenues are difficult to collect partly because of changing institutional arrangements in marketing but also because compliance is low and difficult to enforce given the weak staffing resources and equipment of most district authorities. At the same time, there is a perception that political interference has hampered revenue collection efforts. Moreover, it has been argued that central government takes for itself most of the productive revenue sources — and all the by-laws must be approved by central government.

Some districts are too small to be efficient, but although they vary in terms of area and population size, they have the same local government administrative structure and overheads. The multiplication of administrative units has increased the demand for personnel experienced in local government affairs so that cannot be met from existing sources of supply. The political demands for the creation of new administrative districts and the ease with which these are granted is unlikely to be matched by growing numbers of trained local government personnel.

There is legislation — for instance, Act No. 9 of 1982, which stipulates the sources of finances for local authorities, and Act No. 10 of 1982 for staff matters etc. — which is supposed to guide local government practice. However, some activities on the ground are actually directed by circulars that often contradict what has been stipulated in the legislation, thus causing inconsistencies and weakening institutional functioning. There are many agencies dealing with local government issues (Ministries, PMO, LGSC, RC, DC), which leads to confusion when it comes to assessing capacity and finding ways to develop it.

4.3.1.2 *Ward and village level*

There is a serious discrepancy between the stated responsibilities of these levels of government, as outlined in the Acts, and the quality of their staff and facilities. Wards and villages are staffed by executive officers, most of whom are unqualified. There is no effective or worthwhile office structure or office equipment.

4.3.2 *Initiatives towards reforms*

Local government and regional administration reforms are currently under discussion. Since 1984, two parallel systems have operated. At the regional level the administrative system is centred around the Regional Development Director (RDD), with a fully fledged departmental structure linked down to the district level through a Regional Development Committee (RDC) to the District Development Committee (DDC) chaired by the Regional Commissioner and the District Commissioner respectively. The DDC is a statutory forum for the co-ordination of plans and programmes prepared at different levels within each district, while the RDC consolidates district plans into one regional plan and apportions responsibility and resources between the regional and district levels for programme implementation. A consolidated regional plan is then submitted to the central planning institutions for funding.

At the local government level a separate system operates whereby all the council plans go through the council economic and finance committee before they are adopted by the full council. The council planning cycle is based on a calendar year while that of the central government runs from July to June.

Under current reform proposals, both the RDC and DDC will be abolished, implying that there will no longer be a separate central government plan at the district level and that the regional level will not have a planning function. Rather, it will co-ordinate all the district council plans through a secretariat to be established and headed by regional administrative secretary under the overall supervision of the Regional Commissioner, a political appointee of the President. The secretariat will consist of line officers, who will link down to the district council and their respective operations departments and up to the relevant line or technical Ministries. Under this proposed structure, virtually all the planning and execution will be carried out at the district level through the district council.

This reform has a number of implications. First, it means that the regional administrative structure will be scaled down to a small co-ordinating unit. In addition, the region will no longer have a development budget. This in turn means that professionals previously at the regional level could be deployed to the district councils where all operations will take place.

With regard to personnel management, technical Ministries will retain their role of professionally developing staff in their respective fields of competence. However, all such staff will be accountable to their employers — the district councils — in their day-to-day operations. There is, nevertheless, some ambivalence as to how this system of accountability will operate, particularly when local authorities are not yet financially independent. This raises a further question of distribution of revenue sources between the central government and local authorities.

Quite obviously there are daunting tasks ahead for local government reform. First, there is the need to step up efforts to train and retrain staff for local government service. Second, there is the need for capacity building at regional level for co-ordination (not interference). Third, there is the need to consider applying viability criteria and reconstituting councils into viable units. Fourth, there is concern about the low level of education of councillors who must now shoulder greater responsibilities and exercise more power over officers.

The incentive environment is currently characterised by:

- poor pay packages and unattractive schemes of service that fail to reflect the cost of living;
- lack of a clear or up-to-date wage and fringe benefits policy;
- poor working environment with inadequate and outdated equipment; and
- uncertainty in career development.

4.4 CAPACITY BUILDING: WHAT IS TO BE DONE

4.4.1 DEVELOPMENT OF HUMAN RESOURCES

The regions and local councils are allocated a relatively small share of total funds from central government to finance their recurrent and development expenditures, leaving only limited resources for human resource development. In the midst of pressures to deliver urgently needed goods and services, councillors give staff development low priority compared to other activities.

Local authorities lack the ability and resources to train staff. So far most have been unable to offer short courses to keep their staff abreast of recent developments in management, etc. They mostly depend on the Local Government Service Commission (LGSC), although its training budget was below 30% for the four financial years 1992-1996, as shown in Table 9 below.

There is a shortage of appropriate local government-oriented training institutions. Currently there are two institutes for training of local government cadres — the Institute of Development Management (IDM) in Morogoro, and Hombolo Local Government Training Institute in Dodoma. The curriculum at IDM needs revising so as to reflect the needs of local government, while Hombolo has never yet offered training since its establishment under Act No. 26 of 1994.

TABLE 9: TRAINING REQUIREMENTS & ACTUAL DISBURSEMENT IN LOCAL GOVERNMENT SERVICE COMMISSION

Year	Requirements (T.shs.)	Actual (T.shs.)	Percentage (%)
1992/1993	240,000,000	65,145,400	27.14
1993/1994	256,400,000	62,794,000	24.4
1994/1995	360,600,000	106,700,000	29.5
1995/1996	380,000,000	80,700,000	20.2

Source: Local Government Service Commission

4.4.2 POLICY ENVIRONMENT

There should be clearer policies related to the required level of capacity in local government, the rationalisation of its functions and nourishing it to meet future challenges. There is a need for better co-ordination of central government policy decisions that affect local authorities under one lead agency, to reduce conflicts in priorities and duplication of functions, and to increase efficiency in the follow-up of the implementation of projects and programmes. Revenue allocation should correspond with the responsibilities at both local and regional level. Incentive packages, (i.e., salaries, pension benefits and other emoluments) should reflect the pressures and requirements of the job. In addition, career development should be systematised and working facilities should be improved. Councillor/executive staff working relations should be re-examined to define more clearly the demarcation of authority.

4.5 THE ROLE OF DONORS

4.5.1 Donor activities

4.5.1.1 *Current involvement*

Donors are currently involved in many councils covering a number of sectors. This includes the Dutch, who are involved in district development programmes in 13 districts, the Irish in three districts, the World Bank in nine municipalities, etc.

4.5.1.2 *Problem Areas*

There are several problems that can be observed. To begin with, too much funding is spent on salaries and upkeep of own staff; and there are prioritisation problems, in that the activities donors are involved in do not always reflect the conditions and wishes of locals. Differing approaches are used by donors to tackle similar problems in different districts, reflecting more the whims and background of the donor staff than specific characteristics of different communities. The sustainability of projects and programmes is also questionable, both in terms of funding and the involvement of local people in the creation, implementation and execution of programmes.

4.5.1.3 *Opportunities*

Opportunities for fruitful donor assistance lie in exercising measures that will ensure relevance and adaptability of programmes and sustainability. These include making greater use of local people in various leadership and managerial capacities, involving the people concerned in priority setting, and the scrutiny of expatriate staff by local authorities to ensure the kind of donor assistance that is both useful and beneficial to the communities.

5. CAPACITY IN THE PRIVATE SECTOR

5.1 INTRODUCTION

Three decades have elapsed since Tanzania embraced a socialist path of development. With the best of intentions, socialist policies by and large failed to achieve their principle goal of building a sustainable, self-reliant economy that assures distributive and social justice. Between 1967 (when the Arusha Declaration was promulgated) and the early 1980s, there was entrenchment of the role of the State as entrepreneur and as an instrument of economic regulation and control. The pillars of this State were the One Party, the State-owned enterprise sector and the bureaucracy. In this dispensation, the organised private sector (trade and industry) was not only marginalised, but through deliberate policy (the Arusha Declaration's 'Leadership Code') it remained predominantly owned by a national racial minority. Representative bodies of the private sector lacked a voice and had little impact in terms of influencing economic policy making.

At the level of the 'unorganised' private sector, particularly peasant agriculture, socialist policies led to the erosion of private initiative through the implementation of *ujamaa* and 'villagisation'. The co-operatives — which had been the peasants' own instruments for promoting their collective objectives — were 'socialised' by the State, brought under the control of the Party and later, in the early 1970s, abolished in the name of promoting village-based collectivisation of both production and marketing. The result of these policies was a general decline in agricultural production and growing poverty in rural Tanzania.

Thus, for a critical period of over 20 years, Tanzania failed to mobilise its human and institutional capacities and resources effectively. Since 1986, however, the country has embarked on broad-based economic reforms and new thinking has emerged, which views the private sector as the driving force for social and economic transformation. Yet, largely because of the socialist past and the ambivalence characteristic of economies in ideological transition, the private sector remains fragile and fragmented, its ownership structure in larger scale trade and industry levels stratified along racial lines, which could spark social tension. At the level of agricultural production, in spite of the reinstatement of co-operatives in 1984, peasant agriculture remains rain dependent and of low productivity, based on the hoe, poor seed varieties, lack of chemicals, lack of extension services, etc.

Mainly because of its marginalisation, no serious research on the private sector has been undertaken, and consequently information about its size and composition remains limited and imprecise. There is excessive business secrecy, fuelled by unscrupulous and unethical business practices and tax evasion, which contributes to a serious lack of reliable data about the private sector. Company records compiled by the Ministry of Industries and Trade (MIT) indicate that there were about 27,000 private businesses registered over a period of 63 years, from 1932 to 1995. Due to poor record keeping and follow up it is not known, with any accuracy, how many of these firms are still operating. However, 8603 of these firms were registered in the four-year period between 1992 and 1995. The recent sharp increase of private sector corporate formation points to a re-emergence of private business activity.

Tanzanians of Asian origin make up less than 2% of the country's total population. They control a major proportion of private businesses. The indigenous African majority, who account for over 98% of the total population, operate mainly within the informal small business sectors and smallholder farming.

Development of the private sector in the rural areas, where the majority of indigenous Africans live, is constrained by the poor performance of the co-operative unions, most of which are insolvent, heavily indebted and unable to perform their roles of promoting agricultural marketing and assuring effective farm inputs distribution. Current problems of the co-operative unions are largely rooted in their socialisation and subsequent abolition in favour of village-based socialist co-operatives and Crop Marketing Authorities. Though now independent of the State, the co-operative unions suffer from poor management and fail to have a positive impact in assisting the capacity building and transformation of peasant agriculture.

5.2 CONSTRAINTS TO CAPACITY BUILDING IN THE PRIVATE SECTOR

Banking and financial systems still remain weak, with a large State-owned sector that is being restructured. By 1991, when the government first introduced the Financial Sector Reform Programme, the country's financial system was described as one of the least developed in Sub-Saharan Africa. Before reform, the financial system was characterised by a lack of competition. By 1991, there were only 14 financial institutions in the country. Of these, 12 were State-owned including the National Bank of Commerce, which controlled 88% of the national market for loans and deposits and accounted for 83% of total commercial banking assets. The banking system was constrained by a government-administered credit policy, which fixed ceilings on bank lending and deposits, interest rates and exchange rates.

Although considerable progress has been made in liberalising the financial sector, there is still limited effective competition in the market. Even today, private businesses operate within a financial system that is more supply- than demand-driven and is not responsive to market needs. Credit for investment and for working capital is in short supply because equity and term financing institutions are restructuring their non-performing portfolios and cleaning up their balance sheets. It will take time before these institutions recover enough to have adequate funds for term lending.

Lending to agricultural production, particularly for peasant agriculture, is more or less non-existent. There is an absence of rural financial intermediaries that could extend credit for agriculture transformation. Commercial banks have found it more profitable to invest in Treasury Bills, thus crowding out productive investments from accessing adequate working capital, and even the new private sector banks have been reluctant to lend to the private sector. There is uncertainty about the direction and sustainability of the macroeconomic policy framework, which is overly dependent on external funding.

There is still apprehensiveness about the genuineness of government commitment to developing the private sector. While the mistrust of private entrepreneurship embodied in the *ujamaa* ideology is no longer vocal, vestigial anti-business attitudes remain. These find expression, for example, in the undue delays to obtain the necessary approvals and licenses to establish private businesses. It normally takes about 30 days to process an investment application in Hong Kong or the Republic of Ireland. In Tanzania, it may take six months, or even longer.

Ambivalence is also observed in government policy with regard to the reform of, and respect for, property rights, to the exercise of administrative powers by State agencies and the enforceability of contracts. Tanzania lacks a coherent legal code governing private business. According to a 1991 study on the constraints to private sector development, business activity in the city of Dar es Salaam alone is governed by six statutes, 12 by-laws, 15 regulations, 11 ordinances, seven notices and one rule. The complexity and expensiveness of the legal environment for private business is partly to blame for the large number of entrepreneurs, especially small-scale indigenous Tanzanians, who remain in the informal sector.

Another source of difficulty is the unreliability of public services, particularly economic infrastructures including water, transport, energy and telecommunications, and public social services. The declining standard of education, at all levels, inhibits improved enterprise management and results in continued dependence on expatriate recruitment. The education system does not fit the needs of the labour market. In the pursuit of equality, emphasis was placed on the rapid expansion of primary education without matching resources to ensure quality of output. Secondary and tertiary education was de-emphasised. The education system failed to meet the emerging needs for science and technology, business management and entrepreneurship.

There is an absence of an equity capital market that can fund private sector growth through equity. Tanzania still does not have equity markets, which could facilitate the mobilisation of savings for long-term investment. These markets are in the process of being formed, but the culture of family-owned businesses, rather than publicly held firms, continues to be pervasive.

The dominance of Tanzanians of Asian origin in the ownership and control of the organised private sector (manufacturing enterprise and export-import trade) has weakened the impact of the business and business associations. Rent-seeking behaviour and corruption within the bureaucracy and the State-owned regulatory and lending agencies has provided an alternative to action on the part of business actors to improve the regulatory environment. Also, the absence of an effective presence of indigenous African business actors in the membership of business associations has contributed to their present weakness, with business associations failing to be effective voices of their members or of the business community as a whole. A study carried out recently showed that the majority of small and medium size registered firms, particularly those owned by indigenous Africans, do not belong to any business support organisation. They view such organisations, especially the chambers of commerce, as ineffective in rendering services to their members.

The predominantly family-owned private sector in Tanzania has, to some extent, fallen victim to reliance on family management rather than professional management. There is glaring lack of training, particularly for small and medium enterprise capitalists and managers.

5.2.1 ANALYSIS OF POSSIBLE RESPONSES TO THE CONSTRAINTS

As a matter of priority, peasant agriculture must be brought within the realm of capacity building. Agriculture remains the mainstay of Tanzania's economy; presently, over 70% of the Tanzanian population still relies on agriculture as the principal means of livelihood, and it contributes about 50% of GDP. Thus, any efforts directed at poverty eradication and raising the living standards of Tanzanians must give preponderant importance to agricultural transformation. This entails:

(a) improving access to quality primary education;
(b) improving health delivery programmes;
(c) promotion of improved agricultural and animal husbandry methods, including use of better seeds, simple irrigation, fertilisers, plant protection chemicals, and better crop storage;
(d) introduction of well administered credit schemes for agriculture;
(e) improving management of co-operative unions and the crop marketing system;
(f) giving better fiscal incentives for investments in agricultural processing;
(g) promotion of rural banks and community-based savings and credit societies; and
(h) promotion of peasants' service associations linked to a national farmers' association, to lobby for the interests of peasants.

For capacity in trade and industry, the institutionalisation of a formal dialogue between the government and the business sector is needed. There are serious efforts in hand to realise this objective, including a commitment by President Mkapa's government to constitute a Malaysia-type National Business Council, which would comprise selected cabinet ministers, top bureaucrats and representatives of the business sector (public and private) and would be chaired by the Prime Minister.

However, the present fragility of the business associations begs the very objectivity of constructive dialogue and partnership with the government.

Ironically, whilst the business community would welcome such a medium for dialogue as a contribution to building its own capacity, it is faced with a 'chicken and egg' type of dilemma. Dialogue should be underpinned by capacity for policy dialogue within the business community, which, unfortunately, is presently weak. To be able to turn the planned National Business Council into a forceful organ of dialogue, it is imperative that the business community mobilises itself into a strong and cohesive network of associations representing the broad spectrum of business actors in the economy.

It is essential that strong and sustainable national bodies representing all business interests be established. The strength and sustainability of such organs hinges on financial autonomy, away from the present unhealthy and unsustainable dependency on a few benefactors, largely the successful Asian Tanzanian-owned enterprises. One possibility would be for all business license holders to pay a statutory fee (determined on the basis of the value of each business license) to fund the national bodies; however, that would have the disadvantage of introducing a non-voluntary basis for the associations. The second need for capacity building in the business sector is the development of entrepreneurial capacity, which will require squarely addressing issues such as:

(a) provision of entrepreneurship training facilities to nascent small and medium scale entrepreneurs;
(b) the need to put in place adequate venture capital financing institutions which are focused on financing small and medium scale ventures;
(c) the development of broader ownership of privatised State-owned enterprises, as well as large family-owned businesses, through a stock market or stock exchange; and
(d) re-orientation of the education system to make it respond to market needs, with a focus on providing the kind of education and training which cultivates the entrepreneurial spirit and self employment.

Developing national confidence in a private sector, which is still widely viewed as an instrument of exploitation and enrichment by a racial minority, is a critical element in building private sector capacity. A deliberate move away from exclusively family-owned enterprises, towards establishing publicly-held companies, would significantly help to develop a more positive public view of the private sector. However, given the existing tax regime, the prudential accounting rules of disclosure required for publicly-held companies can be an inhibiting factor. As an incentive to and prerequisite for the shift, the tax system should be reformed to make it more conducive to voluntary compliance and truthful disclosure of business affairs.

In the age of globalisation and competitiveness, the capacity to access state of the art (yet relevant) technologies and export markets information, and meet international standards, particularly over the quality and prices of manufactured goods, are critical requirements for national economic growth. In turn, the capacity for research and development is the vehicle for improved quality, product diversity and new product out-turns, for agriculture, trade and industry. The achievement of these capacities depends on:

(a) the private sector being willing to recruit highly trained engineering and science graduates;
(b) reducing dependence on debt characteristics of family ownership predominance and attracting new equity through public share offerings and building the financial strength to acquire improved technologies and boost competitiveness;
(c) promoting collaboration with national research and development institutions and universities;
(d) striking strategic alliances with foreign firms which enjoy global and regional outreach; and
(e) entering into joint ventures with foreign firms which have experience with newer technologies, and have proven management and market access.

More generally, what constitutes an environment conducive to private sector capacity building? It is not enough to simply refer to a stable macroeconomic policy framework — stable exchange rates, market-determined interest rates, controlled inflation and policies that promote free markets. Whilst these are important, there are other critical questions, such as:

(a) Is there a development vision that clearly articulates the ideological path of socio-economic development wherein the private sector is to play a leading role?
(b) Is the legal and regulatory regime responsive to, and supportive of, a new market-oriented environment?
(c) Is the bureaucracy sufficiently sensitive to the needs of private sector-led development?
(d) Are public resources being allocated to those areas that promote private sector growth and viability?
(e) Is the public being informed about the changing roles of the public and the private sectors?
(f) Are tax policies and the tax collection machinery in tune with the challenges of regenerating industries, promoting new investments and external trade, discouraging rent-seeking activities and promoting private sector participation in entrepreneurship training, research and development?

5.3 NGOs AND CIVIC GROUPS

NGOs play an increasingly important social role, with new institutions being created to provide for needs that are not being met by either the market or the public sector. Voluntary organisations provide some services that the government would otherwise have to provide. Furthermore, in the process of democratisation, some organisations play the role of representing the interests of particular segments of society in a pluralistic decision-making process.

Civic organisations are established by individuals or groups of individuals with various social and economic goals, operating as not-for-profit organisations. Some are established through the influence of the government. Others are established through donor influence.

According to the 1994 directory of NGOs in Tanzania, produced by TANGO, there are 527 NGOs out of which 483 are National NGOs and 44 are International NGOs. The local NGOs are in the following fields: AIDS (5), Education (10), Environment (54), Health (34), Professions (50), Religious (54), Social and Economic Development (216) and Women and Youth (60). NGOs, as pressure groups, can influence local, national, regional and international issues.

A number of educational and religious NGOs started before Independence — the NGO directory includes some established in 1959. Others were formed as a response to recent social problems, such as AIDS, or as part of contemporary international policy concern, such as the environmental NGOs. Many reflect the influence of external NGOs or donor financing.

Many local NGOs are weak because of the difficulty of raising funds to sustain their activities. A number of NGOs operating in the country are affiliates of NGOs registered elsewhere, leading to erosion of autonomy in priority setting. This can be a hindrance to the development of local capacity. There is a tendency to choose activities that are amenable to support from outside rather than those which are important to local citizens. This aspect is important, since NGO lobbies can determine the future path of the economic and social development of the country.

In the past, policies in Tanzania have tended to neglect the importance of service institutions other than the government-owned institutions, envisaging that the government could provide all social and economic services. Very little attention was therefore paid to exploring avenues and opportunities available for the NGOs in the development process.

Although NGOs have tried to fill various gaps existing in the social and economic structures of the country, to date NGOs have not been well represented in planning and policy-making organs established by the government. In a more pluralistic, decentralised economy and political system, NGOs are likely to be increasingly important in terms of delivering services, forming and reflecting public opinion and representing the interests of various groups in society.

6. PRIMARY AND SECONDARY EDUCATION AND VOCATIONAL TRAINING

This chapter reviews the status of basic education in Tanzania and points out the problems which, if not adequately addressed, will seriously affect capacity building in Tanzania. Basic education is taken to encompass pre-school, primary education, adult education, secondary education and teacher training, as well as vocational training.

Basic education underwent momentous changes during the years 1980-1995. In the late 1970s and early '80s Tanzania made considerable progress in achieving Universal Primary Education (UPE) and eradicating illiteracy, but these achievements have been seriously eroded due to economic difficulties. Weak management has exacerbated the financial resources constraint. An obvious example of the deterioration is the decline in the gross enrolment ratio in primary education, which reached the peak of 98% in 1981. In 1996, this ratio has fallen to about 70%. Similar deterioration is observed in adult literacy, which reached 90% in 1980 and is now estimated to be around 60%. Secondary schools admit only 15% of those who complete primary education. Tanzania faces the great danger of lagging behind in its development efforts if basic education is not given the importance it deserves.

6.1 THE CURRENT SITUATION

6.1.1 Pre-school and Adult Education

Before enrolment into primary education, some children, particularly in urban areas, attend pre-school facilities — a nursery school, accommodating children of ages three to four, followed by a formal pre-school establishment admitting children of ages five to six. In rural areas however, most children go straight into regular primary schools.

The pre-school stage can be important and, depending on how well it is undertaken, further educational experience may be influenced by it. For this reason, in the recently adopted Education and Training Policy, pre-school education has been given prominence, with a view to it becoming a requirement for all children. However, less than 10% of all eligible children were attending nursery and regular pre-school establishments.

Adult education in the late 1970s and early '80s made an important contribution to almost wiping out illiteracy. With the resurgence of illiteracy, there is a need to revitalise the programme.

6.1.2 PRIMARY EDUCATION

Currently there are about 12,000 primary schools in Tanzania. The total number of pupils in primary schools increased from 827,984 in 1970 to 3,872,473 in 1995, the most rapid increase taking place during the adoption of UPE (1970-1980) as the table below shows.

TABLE 10: PRIMARY EDUCATION PUPILS

Year	Total Enrolment (Std.I-VII)
1970	827,984
1975	1,532,953
1980	3,483,944
1985	3,160,145
1990	3,379,000
1995	3,872,473

Source: Ministry of Education

The quality of education at the primary school level has undergone significant changes during the last 30 years, particularly from 1975 when UPE was launched. Previous to that, the schools were well supplied by properly qualified teachers. With the introduction of UPE, the number of schools and enrolment increased rapidly, and as a result a vast programme of teacher training was launched. That programme admitted Std. VII leavers for a formal one-year teacher-training programme, instead of the regular Form IV leavers' two-year teacher-training programme.

Given the shortage of properly qualified teachers, the standards of education started to decline. There were, however, significant variations in quality between different schools. Those schools which retained most of the older generation of better qualified teachers continued to perform well, whereas the newly opened schools with less-qualified and less-experienced teachers performed poorly. These variations have continued until today, and several schools have never produced even one pupil qualified for entry into a secondary school.

Declining performance placed in question the capacity of primary schools to produce the right quality of students to enter into the next stage of the education ladder (secondary schools). Poor performance has affected both rural and urban primary schools, but the problem is worse in rural areas since there is a tendency for better qualified teachers to teach in urban schools or in areas close to urban centres. Furthermore, in those areas students benefit from tutorial lessons provided outside the regular school programme.

In addition to the declining quality of teachers (due to inadequate training), the deterioration of basic infrastructure, coupled with shortage of teaching materials, has contributed significantly to the decline. Many primary schools lack adequate classrooms and have to share the few rooms available in double or treble sessions, reducing the amount of time available for effective teaching and learning. In 1994, the shortfall of classrooms was estimated to be about 40%. Secondly, even where classrooms are available, there may be inadequate or insufficient desks. It is estimated that about 50% of pupils do not have desks. Thirdly, teaching materials such as books, chalk and apparatus are in seriously short supply. Currently it is estimated that the pupil/book ratio is about 13:1 as opposed to the target of 3:1. The table below illustrates the under-supply of basic facilities for the delivery of primary school education.

TABLE 11: PERMANENT BUILDINGS AND FURNITURE IN PRIMARY SCHOOLS IN 1994 (ALL REGIONS)

Type of building or furniture	Required (1)	Actual (2)	Shortage (3)	(3) as % of (1)
Classrooms	85,844	51,688	43,223	39.9
Staff houses	102,864	24,830	81,593	79.3
Toilets	148,044	43,261	104,783	70.8
Desks	1,658,064	810,646	865,608	52.2
Tables	183,487	71,207	112,280	61.2
Chairs	193,343	62,098	131,245	67.9
Cupboards	114,522	29,654	84,868	74.1

Source: Ministry of Education

Due to seriously deteriorated conditions, the dropout rates in Stds I and II average about 6.6% and a proportion of pupils in Std. VII do not even attempt the final examination that would qualify them to join a secondary school. The situation has become progressively worse; for example, whereas in 1980 only 0.8% did not appear for the final examination, 8% of the pupils did not sit the exam in 1995.

The Government acknowledges the critical role played by primary education, and has instituted several remedial measures, including:

(a) inviting greater participation of parents and the community in school management;
(b) increasing in-service teacher training and upgrading standards in teacher training institutions;
(c) providing special allowances to teachers as an incentive to improve performance;
(d) encouraging donors to allocate more resources to this sector;

(e) allowing the private sector to open and run schools; and
(f) reviewing the curriculum to adjust to changing circumstances and to the practical needs of the localities where the schools are situated.

6.1.3 SECONDARY EDUCATION

Secondary education is the level that prepares students for career selection. At this level, each student has the option to decide to proceed with further studies or join special career-related programmes that lead to specific professions. The students' performances at this stage play a very important role in determining their prospects. Secondary education in Tanzania takes place at two levels. The first level is popularly known as Ordinary Level and normally takes four years after completion of Std. VII. At the end of four years, an Ordinary Level School Certificate Examination is undertaken, determining entry to the second level, which is the Advanced Level. The Advanced Level takes two years, covering Forms V and VI. The best performers at this level join universities and other institutions of higher learning; the rest join different professional programmes depending on availability.

Given that it is at this level that students prepare to join the professional labour market, this is where a major concern for capacity building lies. How many students actually reach this level? Does their performance allow them to join the critical professions necessary for rapid social and economic development? Before these issues are discussed further, a brief survey of the numbers qualifying to reach this level is in order.

6.1.3.1 *Secondary education: Ordinary Level*

In Tanzania the transition rate (graduation from primary to secondary education) is currently very low, even compared with neighbouring countries. It is estimated that the Net Enrolment Ratio (NER) for secondary education was only about 6%, compared to an average of about 15% for Sub-Saharan Africa. The table below depicts development from 1963 to 1995.

TABLE 12: PRIMARY SCHOOL LEAVERS & FORM I SELECTIONS 1963-1995

YEAR	STD./VII/VII LEAVERS	PUBLIC	%	PRIVATE	%	TOTAL	%
1963	17042	4972	29.2	0	0.0	4972	29.2
1964	20348	5302	26.1	458	2.3	5760	28.3
1965	29367	5842	20.2	2329	7.9	8271	28.2
1966	41083	6377	15.5	2591	6.3	8968	21.8
1967	47981	6635	13.8	2610	5.4	9245	19.3
1968	58872	6989	11.9	2511	4.3	9500	15.1
1969	60545	7149	11.8	3021	5.0	10170	16.8
1970	64630	7350	11.4	3254	5.0	10604	16.4
1971	70922	7780	11.0	3667	5.2	11447	16.1
1972	87777	7956	9.1	4379	5.0	12335	14.1
1973	106203	8165	7.7	4964	4.7	13129	12.4
1974	119350	8472	7.1	5114	4.3	13586	11.4
1975	137559	8680	6.3	5786	4.2	14466	10.5
1976	156114	8659	5.5	6590	4.2	15249	9.8
1977	169106	8706	5.1	7165	4.2	15871	9.4
1978	185293	8720	4.7	8467	4.6	17187	9.3
1979	193612	8908	4.6	6677	3.4	15585	8.0
1980	212446	8913	4.2	7095	3.3	16008	7.5
1981	357816	9178	2.6	7988	2.2	17166	4.8
1982	419829	9241	2.2	8469	2.0	17710	4.2
1983	454604	9899	2.2	9606	2.1	19505	4.3
1984	649560	10077	1.6	11745	1.8	21822	3.4
1985	429194	10881	2.5	12626	2.9	23506	5.5
1986	380096	11721	3.1	15709	4.1	27430	7.2
1987	380758	14626	3.8	18007	4.7	32633	8.6
1988	347978	15675	4.5	20789	6.0	36464	10.5
1989	267744	18551	6.9	23585	8.8	42136	15.7
1990	306656	19673	6.4	27554	9.0	47227	15.4
1991	383427	19282	5.0	29027	7.6	48309	12.6
1992	346514	21531	5.5	25703	7.4	44896	13.0
1993	363404	21531	5.9	26965	7.4	48496	13.3
1994	370534	24321	6.6	28657	7.7	52819	14.3
1995	386584	28412	7.3	28498	7.4	56910	14.7

Source: Basic Education Statistics in Tanzania (BEST)

As the figures show, the transition rates between 1963 to 1995 have undergone significant variations over the period, ranging from 29.2% in 1963 to the low 3.4% in 1984 and picking up again to above 15% in 1989 and 1990 and declining slightly to 12.6% in 1991. From 1992, the transition rate began to increase and was about 14% in 1995. The main factors causing these trends can be easily explained.

Immediately after Independence, the Government took over most secondary schools that were run by private and religious institutions. These were very few — the total number of students joining Form I was less than 5000 in 1963. The policy of taking over schools was to enable free access and entry for all qualifying students to secondary schools regardless of religion.

The other issue of interest at that time was the small base of the education system. The number of pupils leaving Std.VII in 1963 was only 17,042, while those entering secondary school numbered only 4972. The number of pupils leaving primary school in 1995 had multiplied to over 3.8 million. Following the move towards UPE in the late 1970s and early '80s, the large numbers of Std. VII school leavers had to fight for the limited number of secondary school places, which could only accommodate 3.4% of Std.VII in 1984. In response, independent agencies were encouraged to expand secondary education, and there was an effort by the Government to expand vocational training to absorb a significant number of Std.VII school leavers.

6.1.3.2 *Efforts to introduce specialisation at secondary school level*

Measures were implemented by the Government to improve the marketability and relevance of secondary education in the job market, through specialised further training, beginning in the mid-1980s. Several secondary schools were designated to provide special subjects in addition to regular generalised academic subjects. Specialisations included technical subjects, commercial and home economics, and agriculture.

The success of the specialisation approach has not been very easy to quantify, particularly given that employment opportunities have fallen far short of the number of Form IV leavers. The skills acquired are claimed by employers to be inadequate for direct entry to the labour market. At the same time, further training opportunities are severely limited in the designated post-secondary school institutions.

6.1.3.3 *Expansion of secondary school enrolment*

In order to increase secondary school enrolment, and following the success of the UPE programme, the Government stepped up efforts to encourage the private sector and NGOs to open and manage secondary schools. This effort yielded significant results as demonstrated above. From 1983 the enrolment in public and private schools was more or less equal. Thereafter, the enrolment in private secondary schools has consistently exceeded enrolment in public schools.

From the statistics available, in 1995 there were a total of 595 secondary schools. Among these, 336 were private schools while 259 were public secondary schools. A similar proportion is reflected in secondary school enrolment. A total of 183,659 students were enrolled in secondary schools in 1995 — out of these,

100,037 or 55% were enrolled in private secondary schools. This trend is expected to continue as the Government continues to face resource constraints.

6.1.3.4 *Secondary Education: Advanced Level*

Places available at the advanced level (A-Level) of secondary education are very limited. The transition rate from Form IV to Form V is yet very low, as shown by Table 13, below.

TABLE 13: TRANSITION TO A-LEVEL

Year	No. of students in Form IV (1)	No. of students in Form V (2)	(2) as % of (1)
1970	6,713	1,506	22.4
1975	8,183	1,865	22.8
1980	15,237	1,887	12.4
1985	17,200	2,896	16.8
1990	28,842	5,258	18.2
1995	38.266	6,875	18.0

As can be seen, less than 20% of those who complete Ordinary Level secondary education find a place at the Advanced Level, after which they are eligible to attend a university or other institution of higher learning. The absolute numbers of those entering Form V have increased from 1,506 students in 1970 to 6,875 in 1995 (about a four-fold increase); the number of students completing Form IV has increased over six times during the same period. If one compares the number of students who complete primary education and those who are eligible to enter university, the transition rates are very low.

TABLE 14: TRANSITION FROM STD.VII TO A-LEVEL

Year	Students in Std. VII (1)	Students in Form I (2)	Students in Form V (3)	3 as % of 1
1970	65,624	10,604	1,506	2.3
1975	138,145	14,466	1,865	1.4
1980	212,446	16,008	1,887	0.9
1985	429,194	23,506	2,896	0.7
1990	313,140	47,227	5,258	1.7
1995	420,143	53,698	6,875	1.6

6.1.4 Vocational Training

Interest in vocational training came about in response to the growing phenomenon of Std. VII leavers whose formal academic careers appeared to have ended, while the economy needed artisan skills. One vocational training school was established in Dar es Salaam. When graduates of the vocation-training centre were few, they were quickly absorbed by the then growing manufacturing and construction sectors. The Government undertook to expand these centres to other parts of the country, with plans to establish a vocational training centre in every district; 70% of the districts were covered.

Following the expansion, the popularity of vocational schooling waned. The major reason was that, although the skills they developed were potentially very useful, the slow expansion of the economy and the market for such skills resulted in graduates of these institutions remaining unemployed and thus becoming demoralised.

It is expected that, as the economy revives, the demand for the skills acquired from vocational training institutions will increase. The challenge now is to modernise and improve the content of the vocational training curriculum so that it continues to be relevant to the changing job market.

6.2 PROBLEMS AND CONSTRAINTS TO CAPACITY BUILDING IN BASIC EDUCATION

In order to begin to restore the lost ground in the sector, the Government set out new targets, which were to be reached by the year 2000. Most targets were not reached. It is the assessment of the difficulties of reaching these targets that demonstrates the constraints that may be expected.

6.2.1 Human Resources

In primary education, the target was to reach gross enrolment ratio of 98% (this is equivalent to the UPE level reached in 1981) by the year 2000. However, the current enrolment ratio is about 70%. Taking into account the situation depicted in Table 11, it is obvious that more classrooms are required as well as more teaching materials, etc. Most importantly however, it has been estimated that about 51,000 additional teachers will be required — there is no way that this can be achieved in a short period of time. This does not include other human resources categories responsible for putting in place the required physical structures, etc.

Similarly for secondary education, the target was to achieve the transition rate of 20% by the year 2000, compared with the rate of about 14%. This target required an average annual increase in the enrolment rate of about 14%. There is a current shortage of secondary school teachers, and additional classes will be required.

If the two targets are put together, then the combined requirements for teachers are enormous and it is unlikely that they could be attained. There is therefore an additional challenge of expanding teacher-training colleges in order to produce the required number of teachers to fulfil the policy target.

As regards vocational training, the main challenge is to produce the right kind of skill mix required by the liberalised and diversified economy. The present approach, whereby the Vocational Education and Training Authority (VETA) takes the entire training responsibility for the economy, should be modified in order to cope with the diversified market.

It is therefore evident that a critical constraint of reaching the capacity targets in both the primary and secondary education subsectors is the capacity to train adequate teachers. Even if trained teachers were available, there would be a financial constraint on their employment.

6.2.2 THE EDUCATION AND TRAINING POLICY

The contribution of the private sector and community groups, particularly in providing secondary education has added to capacity. The licensing of more than 30 private primary schools over the last two to three years is yet another positive step in the new institutional arrangement that is developing to address the challenge of education provision.

In March 1995, the Government adopted the Education and Training Policy. Among other things, the Policy emphasises:

(a) liberalisation of the education system;
(b) increased access and improved quality;
(c) introduction of cost-sharing mechanisms;
(d) increased decentralisation at district and community levels; and
(e) improved management at all levels.

The Policy is at a difficult stage and a special Ministerial Committee has been appointed to oversee its implementation. The Committee is required to elaborate on the mechanisms, including incentives, necessary to realise the objectives of the Policy.

6.3 RESPONSES TO THE PROBLEMS AND CONSTRAINTS

The Government's policy of decentralisation and centralisation has made it possible for others, particularly the private sector and the communities, to expand education delivery and thus increase the basis for national capacity. On the other hand, the policy of cost sharing in the public schools has made additional resources available for delivery improvement and expansion. The private sector and communities are responding by opening new schools. New schools include primary schools, secondary schools and even teacher training colleges — there are now six non-public teacher-training colleges. Donors have responded by continuing support, modifying their programmes to cope with changed circumstances.

There are several challenges that need to be addressed to ensure that the efforts to increase national capacity to deliver education do not create other problems. Two such challenges resulting from liberalisation relate mainly to quality and access to education.

- Quality: The rapid expansion of non-public secondary schools has resulted in a serious shortage of teachers, thus affecting overall quality of education. The new streams being opened are mainly arts-subjects based. It is difficult to expand science subjects because of the shortage of science teachers and the high cost of laboratories and laboratory equipment.

- Access: The first problem of access relates to the geographical location of the new schools. Most non-public secondary schools are located in the better-off regions. The second problem relates to cost sharing, which was introduced in public secondary schools and teacher training colleges, and had increased by 1996/97 to not less than T.shs.60,000, compared with T.shs.15,000 for boarding secondary schools. Teacher training cost nothing in 1995/96. This sharp increase is likely to result in dropouts, particularly among students from low-income families.

With regard to gender inequality, there has been some progress. The World Bank is lending money to fund a pilot girls' scholarship programme, through which eligible primary school girls who qualify (but cannot afford) to enter secondary schools receive special scholarships. So far, about 400 girls are in the programme. Similar will be necessary for all eligible but poor students who cannot afford to pay their way through secondary education.

6.4 PROBLEMS AND OPPORTUNITIES RELATED TO DONOR INTERVENTIONS

The donors have supported basic education all along and indeed the impressive achievements recorded, particularly in the 1970s, were in significant part due to donors' support. Support wavered in the late 1970s and declined further in the '80s, when questions of sustainability and management capacity were confronted.

There have been problems with donor interventions in the support for basic education — donor information regarding the amount of aid and its disbursement is often incomplete, and the choices of which components to support are mostly decided by the donor. In addition, there is no certainty of aid flow, which may in any case be terminated unexpectedly. As with aid to other sectors, much bilateral aid is tied to procurement from the donor country, reducing its effectiveness, and too much aid is tied to technical assistance.

Nevertheless, donor interventions have contributed significantly to the development of basic education in Tanzania. There is significant goodwill on both sides to ensure that past mistakes are not repeated and that sustainable structures are put in places. The Government must clearly spell out its priorities and collaborate with donors to achieve more effective co-ordination of interventions in support of education.

Basic education, and primary education in particular, received high priority in the 1970s and early '80s. The momentum then dissipated and there has since been serious deterioration. That momentum must be revived. The government will have to create the necessary conditions for resource mobilisation and encourage partnership between itself, the private sector, the community and donors.

The problems of the education sector problems will not be solved overnight. In the long term, problems in the sector will be solved when the average income levels of all Tanzanians have adequately increased to support a decent education. The education sector cannot be isolated from the rest of the economy, and there will be limits to its development if other sectors stagnate.

7. TERTIARY EDUCATION AND TRAINING CAPACITY

Problems in tertiary, especially in university, education have been addressed in recent years in a number of studies. In view of the wide range of the reports (listed in the bibliography) it is apparent that there is capacity to analyse problems confronting higher education in Tanzania. Whether or not the recommendations arrived at are (or have been) implemented is a different issue, depending for the most part on the financial and material ability, and willingness, to innovate on the part of both the government and the educational institutions. Some of the major issues from the literature are summarised below.

7.1 MAJOR ISSUES

7.1.1 Low Student Enrolment

Relative to its population and in comparison with neighbouring countries, Tanzania has one of the lowest student enrolment rates into institutions of higher learning, currently recorded at only about 3% of the secondary school population. While, for instance, Kenya has a combined total of around 40,000 university-going students in more than ten universities in the country, Tanzania has only about 6,000, although it has a national population comparable to that of Kenya. The rate of university enrolment in Uganda is similar to that of Kenya, notwithstanding an even smaller national population size. Botswana has a student enrolment of around 3000 from a national population of only 1.5 million. Lagging student enrolment in Tanzania has limited the growth of well-educated entrants in the national labour market, which in the last decade has been increasingly liberalised and is increasingly demanding diverse forms of training.

Higher education enrolment has also suffered from an imbalance in the student intake. In particular, there has been an imbalance in intake between the humanities and liberal arts, on the one hand, and the sciences and science-based subjects on the other, with a balance of 1:0.5 against the sciences. A shortage of scientists and technologists will prolong dependency on the outside world for scientifically trained personnel. A deliberate effort is required at both national and institutional levels to expand the flow of students into the science and technology streams.

In recognition of lagging enrolment and an unbalanced intake into programmes, the Tanzanian government has recently developed a higher education policy. It is designed to address the deficits through the public institutions and to invite private sector participation in higher education provision, including private universities, particularly in disciplines and professional areas not adequately covered by the public institutions.

By 1989, a total of about 3200 graduate teachers had been produced by the University of Dar es Salaam for the 319 secondary schools, 40 teacher training colleges and a number of adult education colleges and centres. By the end of 1993, a total of 4478 had been produced, but secondary school numbers alone had grown to 437 in 1993 and to 491 by 1994. The graduate output was not keeping up with the expansion of schools and the proportion of secondary teachers with university training (only one in three by 1989) was falling.

As for the engineering profession, the Faculty of Engineering had, by 1993, produced a total of about 1900 engineers, a cumulative figure giving a ratio of one UDSM-trained engineer for every three engineers practising in the country (there is only one engineer per 14,500 people in the country). With respect to agriculture, and veterinary and allied professions, Tanzania had, by 1993, produced a combined total of 2053 graduates. This gives a current distribution of one graduate professional per 10,130 clients in the national population, which is clearly inadequate.

TABLE 15: ANNUAL UNIVERSITY ENROLMENTS IN SOME EASTERN, CENTRAL AND SOUTHERN AFRICAN COUNTRIES

Country	Population	Annual university enrolment	Ratio of students per 100,000 in the population
Angola	7.5 million	1,000	13
Botswana	1.5 million	600	40
Kenya	27.0 million	11,000	41
Lesotho	1.7 million	500	29
Malawi	8.4 million	1,000	12
Mozambique	15.0 million	1,500	10
Namibia	1.0 million	1,400	140
Swaziland	0.78 million	500	64
Tanzania	27.0 million	2,000	7
Uganda	18.4 million	3,500	19
Zambia	8.4 million	2,000	24
Zimbabwe	10.5 million	3,000	29
South Africa	35.0 million	85,243	244

Sources: various

7.1.2 GENDER BALANCE

Geographical balance, in terms of access to and representation in higher education institutions, has greatly improved since the 1960s. This has been facilitated by growing public and community awareness of and demand for education, and a quota system for student selection for secondary education in the 1970s and '80s.

It is at the level of gender balance that equity in higher education is still far from achieved, as Table 16 indicates. While the sexes are fairly balanced at the primary school and teacher training levels, the balance tilts in favour of boys at the secondary school level. There is conspicuous male domination at university level (74% male against just 16% female) and even more conspicuously so in technical training programmes (94% male compared to 6% female). At Sokoine University of Agriculture, only 16.7% of the enrolled students are female. At the University of Dar es Salaam, the female proportion is even less, at only 15.8%. Among the faculties at the University of Dar es Salaam, 26.9% of the women are enrolled in education, 22.2% in law, 21.7% in arts and social sciences, 16.3% in commerce and management, 13.5% in science and 3.5% in engineering.

In the light of this imbalance, within its corporate strategic plan for institutional transformation and expansion, the University of Dar es Salaam has given priority to female representation, and aimed to enhance the selection of women candidates beginning from the 1996/97 academic year. The University is proposing to the government that women should have preferential access to loans and public sponsorship.

TABLE 16: TRENDS IN FEMALE ENROLMENT IN EDUCATION AND TRAINING PROGRAMMES IN PROPORTION TO MALE ENROLMENT 1971-95 (%)

Year	Primary	Secondary	Teacher Training	Technical Training	University
1971	39.4	26.6	n/a	n/a	15.9
1975	42.0	26.5	n/a	n/a	10.1
1981	47.7	34.0	42.4	9.2	24.0
1983	48.9	35.0	n/a	11.8	19.6
1985	49.9	36.8	41.1	11.2	16.5*
1987	49.8	39.6	40.9	7.5	15.2
1988	49.7	41.1	41.6	5.2	16.9
1989	49.6	42.6	40.8	6.9	17.1
1990	49.5	41.5	52.7	6.8	21.8
1991	49.4	43.2	44.8	6.5	19.2
1992	49.1	43.4	49.6	6.2	18.6
1993	49.2	43.3	51.1	6.5	16.0
1994	49.4	43.9	50.8	6.6	14.8
1995	n/a	n/a	n/a	5.7	16.7

Sources: Ministry of Education and Culture (1993, 1994, 1995) and Ministry of Science, Technology and Higher Education (1993, 1994, 1995)

n/a Statistics not available:

* This proportion in 1985 is based on student enrolment at the University of Dar es Salaam only, excluding statistics at the then newly established Sokoine University of Agriculture.

7.1.3 FINANCING

Tertiary education (including the universities) has been under-financed; and its position is growing more precarious. Table 17 illustrates the financial position of the University of Dar es Salaam in the last 10 years, with regard to government allocations relative to the university's estimate of its budgetary needs to effectively carry out its mission. Sokoine University of Agriculture has been in no better position financially, and in both universities academic activities have suffered due to lack of funds. Many times teachers and researchers have been forced to improvise, but at the cost of compromising standards and placing in question the meaning of the degrees awarded. To address these financial problems, income generating, cost cutting, cost-recovery and cost sharing have been introduced (e.g., in the University of Dar es Salaam Corporate Plan).

TABLE 17: GOVERNMENT ALLOCATIONS TO THE UNIVERSITY OF DAR ES SALAAM, TANZANIA (1985/86-1995/96)

Fiscal Year	Operating budget presented to government		Amounts received		Grant as % of budget
	T.shs. million	USD million	T.shs. million	USD million	
1985/86	41.89	24.0	325.8	18.6	77.8
1986/87	503.5	15.4	455.5	13.9	90.5
1987/88	821.8	12.8	501.0	7.8	61.0
1988/89	1235.4	12.4	801.3	8.1	64.9
1989/90	2417.6	17.0	1302.7	9.1	53.9
1990/91	4801.5	25.0	2003.7	10.4	41.7
1991/92	6645.9	29.4	2640.5	11.7	39.7
1992/93	9401.3	31.2	3295.6	10.9	35.1
1993/94	8149.1	22.2	3065.9	8.4	37.6
1994/95	10441.9	19.7	3009.9	5.7	28.8
1995/96	14013.7	23.5	6505.2	10.9	46.4

Source: University of Dar es Salaam, administration department.

Note: 1 United States Dollar (USD) = 444 Tanzanian shillings (T.shs.) in October 1993. The general decline in budgetary grants and allocations dates back to the late 1970s and early 1980s. The rapid decline from the mid-1980s becomes more apparent when the statistics in Tanzania shillings (T.shs.) are converted into USD equivalents. The official exchange rates were 1 UDS = 17.47 T.shs. in 1985/86, 32.70(1986/87), 64.26(1987/88), 99.29 (1988/89), 142.50 (1989/90), 192.00 (1990/91), and 301.50 (1992/93), 367.10 (1993/94), 528.76 (1994/95), and 595.51 (1995/96), all as at June of each year.

7.1.4 PROLIFERATION OF UNCO-ORDINATED TERTIARY INSTITUTIONS

In the last 30 years of tertiary education provision, there has been little effective government co-ordination, accreditation or harmonisation of the tertiary institutions. They have proliferated, leading to distortions in academic awards and certification, as well as misleading and unstandardised academic staff designations.

In 1982/83, according to a countrywide survey, there were 42 tertiary (post-secondary) institutions in total. Of these, one was a university, eight were non-university tertiary institutions of higher education and training, and 33 were lower-level, largely vocational tertiary institutions, such as nursing training schools and lower grade teacher training colleges. By 1992, according to another countrywide survey, the number had grown to 142 tertiary institutions, including two universities, 13 non-university tertiary institutions of higher education and 127 lower-level tertiary institutions. The new institutions were established or sponsored by various public, private and governmental agencies, but no co-ordination or mutual consultation was instituted between them. This resulted in duplications, and unstandardised and unaccredited courses and awards.

An unfortunate distortion of academic awards has also arisen within higher education. This has been occasioned by non-university tertiary institutions issuing university level qualifications. Notable among these institutions are the Institute of Development Management (IDM), the Institute of Finance Management (IFM), the Institute of Rural Development Planning (IRDP), and Ardhi Institute (prior to its affiliation to the University of Dar es Salaam as its University College of Land and Architectural Studies [UCLAS], beginning in 1986/97 academic year). Thus, in addition to the certificate, diploma and advanced diploma courses it offers, IDM purports to offer programmes of study leading to the award of a 'Masters degree' as well as a 'postgraduate diploma'. IFM, Ardhi and IRDP have followed suit in offering 'advanced' programmes of study leading to awards classified as 'postgraduate diplomas'.

There is a danger that this proliferation will lead to a devaluation of qualifications and undermine the credibility of awards as a result of the relentless search for, and advertisement of, inflated qualifications and awards. It is this unco-ordinated and wasteful proliferation of tertiary education institutions of unstandardised programme and award structures that the Higher Education Policy recently formulated by the government seeks to control and harmonise. The Education (Amendment) Act No.10 of 1995 and the Accreditation Council for Higher Education Act, 1996, provide for the establishment of a Higher Education Council with powers to rationalise the many and various tertiary education institutions, subjecting them to tests for quality.

7.1.5 Relevance

For this study, the relevance of available training to the end-users (including employers in both public and private firms), to the wider world of work (including industry and other forms of production and service organisation), and to the learners themselves, as workers and personal participants of tomorrow, was explored. Doubts have been raised, particularly with regard to the many and highly unco-ordinated, unstandardised pre-university-level tertiary institutions. Despite the inflation in the award structure and staff designations, many employers report that the actual performance of many graduates has left much to be desired.

At the university level, programmes have been kept under some control through mandatory periodic curriculum reviews by individual faculties (often after every three or five years) and also through inter-university consultations and co-ordination at the levels of the Joint Academic Affairs Committee (JAAC) and the Committee of Vice Chancellors and Principals (CVCP). While quality and sensitivity to international standards have been of paramount concern at university level, there have also been, in the last five years, deliberate efforts by some departments to review and restructure programmes in response to a market and 'demand-driven' orientation. The Faculty of Engineering, for instance, has since 1989 been gauging the market signals through both a national-level impact (tracer) study (1989 and 1995) and a regional market study (1995). While in some cases positive ratings by employers have confirmed the relevancy of programmes offered, low ratings on some issues, such as the graduate's attitude towards other employees and the graduate's adjustment to the job, have informed the Faculty about areas where improvements are required.

Other faculties and institutes at the University of Dar es Salaam and at Sokoine University of Agriculture are similarly reviewing their programmes and levels of resource requirements in order to improve the quality and relevance of their programmes. Over the medium term, the public universities will have to be conscious of possible competition from new private institutions.

7.2 AREAS REQUIRING CORRECTIVE ACTION AND DONOR SUPPORT

Expanded student enrolment

Increased student enrolment into higher education institutions is imperative both to improve public access to higher levels of academic and professional preparation and to lower unit costs. Such expansion could be facilitated by a combination of government sponsorship and loan systems ,and direct fee payment by academically qualified private candidates. Strategies to achieve expanded student enrolment include:

(a) establishment by the government of a revolving fund to mobilise resources for a student loan facility;
(b) initiating scholarship funds to encourage candidates to compete for scholarships;
(c) initiation of a course system under which students accumulate course credits, to allow for an increased student intake based on flexible modular study schedules; and
(d) establishing a semester system to facilitate the option of using course modules.

Increased female student enrolment
This could be facilitated by an offer of an increased number of scholarships specifically for female candidates and/or by instituting quotas in favour of female candidates in selection for scholarship grants. Expanding boarding facilities, including campus or nearby hostels, would ease impediments to female enrolment.

Rationalisation and accreditation of tertiary education institutions
Technical and financial support for the new Higher Education Council could be supplied either directly or through the Ministry of Science, Technology and Higher Education. Tertiary education institutions (public and private) should be audited for the purpose of rationalising them, re-registering, de-registering and/or merging them in accordance with set criteria and standards regarding physical facilities, programmes on offer, staff qualifications, and academic/professional awards.

Rationalisation would allow for a disciplined 'expansion with efficiency' through the concentration of resources on the most effective and relevant education and training programmes, avoiding spreading resources too thinly, as well as encouraging the growth of institutions capable of offering creditable courses and awards that command respect. Rationalisation would serve to arrest the tendency of institutions to discard their original missions in the pursuit of academic prestige. For example, the original tasks of the Institute of Development Management (to train the civil service) and that of the Institute of Finance Management (to train financial managers for government and parastatal financial institutions) have been long neglected in favour of the pursuit of academic status, resulting in weakened practical capacity building within the civil service departments and public financial institutions.

There is also a need to accredit and validate tertiary education/training institutions. This will be a professionally demanding task, requiring appropriate checklists, discriminating questionnaires and tests of institutions' programmes and course standards. In view of the extensiveness and complexity of the rationalisation and accreditation process involved, there is a great need for external support.

Increased public financing
Even if savings are possible through rationalisation, and additional funds are mobilised through fees, a substantial increase in public finance for tertiary education institutions will be necessary if they are to recruit and retain qualified teaching staff and maintain appropriate equipment.

Support for the current university corporate strategic plans and implementation programmes
There is need for donor financial and technical support for universities to implement corporate strategic planning, as initiated by the University of Dar es Salaam. The plan and its implementation involve institutional transformation and administrative restructuring, rationalisation of academic units, selected expansion of facilities for

expanded student intake and staff retraining for a new organisational culture. This is an area where increased government and donor support would be critical well into the early years of the 2000s.

While universities have begun implementing some of the provisions in their strategic plans — such as expansion in student enrolment, admitting private fee-paying candidates and implementing various cost-cutting and income-generating measures — donor agencies and countries could assist them in putting in place critical facilities. These include:

(a) residences for girls, to encourage increased female participation to redress the gender imbalance;
(b) larger capacity lecture theaters, laboratories and multi-purpose auditoriums to accommodate expanded student intakes;
(c) course textbooks and journal subscriptions; and
(d) laboratory equipment and essential chemicals.

Strengthening teaching

Teaching-learning improvement units and clinics need to be revamped and augmented in order to strengthen the pedagogical methods and skills of teaching staff, and technical and administrative staff allied to the teaching process.

As regards staff training and recruitment for higher education institutions, this is currently not as urgent as is qualitative staff development and professional improvement for teachers already deployed. Staff-student ratios are currently too high, basically because there are too few students (e.g., 1:5 at the University of Dar es Salaam and 1:3 at Sokoine University of Agriculture, as compared with 1:15 at Addis Ababa University, 1:14 at Zambia and 1:11 at Swaziland and Zimbabwe). If student enrolment is substantially expanded and the existing staff accorded the necessary working tools, higher education institutions in Tanzania would not need massive training and expanded staff recruitment.

REFERENCES

CHAPTER 2

1. PLANCOMM, Planning Commission Overall Training Needs.
2. Ministry of Finance: Aid Management and Accountability PLANCOMM. Improvement for Tanzania. Prepared by the Aid Management Administration and Aid System (AMACS) Project Team.
3. Ministry of Finance Budget Management Development Programme BMDP (implementation report).
4. Bureau of Statistics, 'Memorandum on the future of the Bureau.'
5. Treasury/DEVPLAN, *A Manual of the Budget Process in Tanzania.*
6. TRA, 'Briefing to the Donor Community on the operationalisation of TRA.' May and April, 1996.
7. Ex-Audit Tanzania, PATID Government Audit project working paper on Training — October 1990.
8. Accountant General Staff Development 1995/96-1997/98.

CHAPTER 3

Baguma, R. (1992) *The Size and Scope of the Civil Service in Tanzania*. Educational Publishers and Distributors.

CSRP (Civil Service Reform Programme) (1992) *A Review of Skill Levels and Skill Gaps of Civil Service Employees.*

CSRP (1995) *Towards Management Performance Improvement in the Tanzania Civil Service: Issues, Action and Implementation Strategies.*

CSRP *Modernisation of Administrative Technologies in Government Operations.*

CSRP (1996) *Vision, Strategy and Action Plan 1996-1999.*

CSRP (1996) *Capacity Building Plan for the Civil Service.*

Nsekela, A. J. (1987) *Salaries Review Commission: Salaries and other Terms and Conditions of the Civil Service*. Report to the Government of the United Republic of Tanzania.

Rugumyamheto, J. A., *Size and Structure of the Civil Service*. Paper for a study commissioned by the CSRP on the Rationalisation and Restructuring of Government Employment.

URT (United Republic of Tanzania) (1994) *Country Report on Population and Development.*

UNDP (United Nations Development Programme) (1994) *Capacity Development: Lessons of Experience and Guiding Principles.*

CHAPTER 4

Boeninger, E. (1991) *Governance and Development: Issues and Constraints*. Proceedings of World Bank Annual Conference on Development Economics, pp. 267-87.

Economic Research Bureau *Tanzania Economic Trends (TET)*. Various issues. University of Dar es Salaam.

Likwelile, S.B. and Mahyenga, N.N. (1993) *Linkages Between Central Government Ministries, Regional Administration and Local Governments. Report No. 1*. Civil Service Reform Programme, Dar es Salaam.

Local Government Legislations (Act. No.7, 8, 9 and 10) of 1982.

Msambichaka L.A. et al. (eds.) (1994) *Development Challenges and Strategies for Tanzania: An Agenda for the 21st Century.* Dar es Salaam University Press, Dar es Salaam.

URT (United Republic of Tanzania), WB (World Bank) and IMF (International Monetary Fund) (1991) *Economic Policy Framework Paper for 1991/92-93-94*, Dar es Salaam.

Wai, D.M. (1995) *The Essence of Capacity Building in Africa*. James S. Coleman African Studies Centre, University of California.

BIBLIOGRAPHY

Bisanda, E.T.N., Yonah, O.M.Z., Nyichomba, B. & Masuha, J.R. (1995) *Regional Market Study*. Faculty of Engineering, UDSM.

Boeninger, E. (1991) 'Governance and Development: Issues and Constraints.' Proceedings of the World Bank Annual Conference on Development Economics (pp. 267-87).

Buberwa, S.B. (1994) *The Labour Market* (Draft). World Bank, Dar es Salaam.

ESAURP (Eastern and Southern African Universities Research Programme) (1987) *University Capacity in Eastern and Southern Africa*. James Currey, London.

ESAURP (1992) *Tertiary Training Capacity*. A Report to the Planning Commission, United Republic of Tanzania. ESAURP, Dar es Salaam.

Galabawa, J.C. (1989) 'Cost-Benefit Analysis of Private Returns to University Schooling in Tanzania.' Ph.D. dissertation. University of Alberta, Canada.

Ishumi, A.G.M. (1990) *Educational Development in Eastern and Southern Africa: A Critical Review of Policy and Practice, 1960s-80s.* VRS Series No. 178. Institute of Developing Economies, Tokyo.

Ishumi, A.G.M. (1994) 'Higher Education in Tanzania: Past Trends and Challenges for the Future' in Msambichaka, L.A., H.P.B. Moshi & F.P. Mtatifikolo, (eds.) *Development Challenges and Strategies for Tanzania: An Agenda for the 21st Century*. Dar es Salaam University Press, Dar es Salaam.

Ishumi, A.G.M. (1994) *30 Years of Learning: Educational Development in Eastern and Southern Africa from Independence to 1990*. IDRC Books, Ottawa.

Lwambuka, L., Mashauri, D., Kissaka, M., Mutagahawaya, B. & Njau, J. (1995) *National Level Impact Study*. Faculty of Engineering, UDSM.

Malekela, G., Ndabi, D. & Cooksey, B. (1990) *Girls' Educational Opportunities and Performance in Tanzania*. TADREG Research Report No. 2. Tanzania Development Research Group (TADREG), Dar es Salaam.

Maliyamkono, T.L. & Bagachwa, M. (1990) *Tertiary Training Capacity in Tanzania: Report on the Planning Commission*. United Republic of Tanzania (URT), Dar es Salaam.

Materu, P.N. & Omari, I.M. (1995) 'Donor Participation in Post-Primary Education and Training in Tanzania.' Consultancy report, World Bank.

Mbilinyi,M.J. et al (1991) *Education in Tanzania with a Gender Perspective*. SIDA, Stockholm.

Mbwette, T.S.A. (1995) 'How Donors and UniversityCo-operation Can Assist in the Enhancement of Research and Development Competence.' Paper for NUFU/OSSREA Seminar, Addis Ababa, Ethiopia, September 25-27.

MoE (Ministry of Education) (1990) *Report of the Committee on the Establishment of the Open University in Tanzania*. MoE, Dar es Salaam.

MoE (1991) *Report on the Establishment of Constituent Colleges of the University of Tanzania*. MoE, Dar es Salaam.

Msolla, P. & Mapunda, O.B. (1990) 'The Role of University Education in Leadership in the 21st Century: Challenges for Tanzania and Africa.' Solicited paper for the Ministry of Science, Technology and Higher Education, Dar es Salaam.

MSTHE (Ministry of Science, Technology and Higher Education) (1990) *Higher and Technical Education Statistics in Tanzania 1988/89*. MSTHE, Dar es Salaam.

MSTHE (1991-95) *Higher and Technical Education Statistics in Tanzania*. MSTHE, Dar es Salaam.

MSTHE (1993) *Proposed National Policy on Technical Education and Training*. MSTHE, Dar es Salaam.

MSTHE (1993) 'The National Science and Technology Policy for Tanzania' (draft).

Mwiria, K. (1992) 'University Governance: Problems and Prospects in Anglophone Africa.' ACTED Technical Paper No.3. World Bank, Washington DC.

Omari, I. M., Materu, P. N. & Mteleka, T. M. (1996) 'Rationalisation of the Tertiary Education and Training Sector in Tanzania: Expansion with efficiency.' Paper prepared for the MSTHE and the World Bank, Dar es Salaam.

Penrose, P. (1992) *Review of Public Expenditure in the Education Sector: The United Republic of Tanzania*. EEC, Cambridge.

SUA (Sokoine University of Agriculture) Council (1989) *The Education System in Tanzania and Problems associated with Low Intake of Students in Higher Institutions of Learning in Tanzania*. SUA, Morogoro.

SUA (1990) *Annual Report on the Activities of Sokoine University of Agriculture.*

SUA (1991-95) *Annual Reports on the Activities of Sokoine University of Agriculture.*

UDSM (University of Dar es Salaam) (1990) *Annual Report on the Activities of the University of Dar es Salaam*. UDSM, Dar es Salaam.

UDSM (1991) *Report of the Steering Committee on University Management Effectiveness Review*. UDSM, Dar es Salaam.

UDSM (1992) *The Vision and Mission of the Faculty of Education*. UDSM, Faculty of Education, Dar es Salaam.

UDSM (1994) *Corporate Strategic Plan: Strategic Development Programme*. UDSM, Dar es Salaam.

UDSM (1995) *Cost-Cutting and Income-Generating, Measures at the University of Dar es Salaam*. UDSM, Dar es Salaam.

UDSM (1995) *Institutional Transformation Programme, UDSM-2000, Facts and Figures*. UDSM, Dar es Salaam.

UDSM (1995) *Cost-Cutting and Income-Generating Measures at the University of Dar es Salaam: Volume I, Proposed Cost-Cutting Measures with Respect to Administrative Personnel*. UDSM, Dar es Salaam.

UDSM (1996) *Institutional Transformation Programme, UDSM-2000: University-level Five Strategic Plan, 1996-2001 (Version No.3)*. UDSM, Dar es Salaam.

URT (1995) *Education (Amendment) Act, No.10, of 1995.*

URT (United Republic of Tanzania) (1993) *The Tanzania Education System for the 21st Century. Report of the Task Force*. MoEC & MSTHE, Dar es Salaam.

URT (1995) *Higher Education Policy*. MSTHE, Dar es Salaam.

World Bank (1995) *Tanzania Social Sector Review*. Dar es Salaam/Washington DC

World Bank (1996) *Post-Primary Education and Training in Tanzania: Investments, Returns and Future Opportunities*. Population and Human Resources Division, Eastern Africa Department.

APPENDIX

MEMBERS OF THE NATIONAL ASSESSMENT TEAM FOR TANZANIA

1. Prof. Samuel. M. Wangwe, Professor of Economics and Executive Director, Economic and Social Research Foundation (Chairman)
2. Mr. Salmon Odunga, Principal Secretary, Ministry of Education and Culture
3. Mr. Francis Zangira, Chief Economist, IPP Ltd.
4. Mr. George Yambesi, Civil Service Reform
5. Mr. Juma Mwapachu, Managing Director, JV Group
6. Prof. Abel Ishumi, Professor of Education and Director of Postgraduate Studies, University of Dar es Salaam
7. Prof. Mark Mwandosya, Professor of Engineering and Director,Center for Energy, Environment, Science & Technology
8. Mr. Mahiza, Director Of Planning, Planning Commission
9. Prof. Joshua Doriye, Deputy Principal Secretary, Prime Minister's Office